Dominic Holmes is a Partner at Mishcon de Reya. He is known for his straightforward, commercial approach to complex employment law issues.

Dominic has over 17 years' experience in advising employers on the legal and practical implications of TUPE across a range of sectors, both within the UK and in the context of multi-jurisdictional projects. He has supported businesses on TUPE issues in matters as varied as global outsourcing exercises, intra-group transfers of undertakings, the sale of businesses out of insolvency and TUPE-related litigation. Dominic has condensed his experience into an accessible, jargon-free book for anyone advising on TUPE or dealing with it in-house.

A Practical Guide to TUPE and Employee Transfers

Core Legal Principles, Tricky Issues and How It Really Works in Practice

A Practical Guide to TUPE and Employee Transfers

Core Legal Principles, Tricky Issues and How It Really Works in Practice

Dominic Holmes

Law Brief Publishing

Published 2023 by Law Brief Publishing, an imprint of Law Brief Publishing Ltd
30 The Parks
Minehead
Somerset
TA24 8BT

www.lawbriefpublishing.com

Paperback: 978-1-914608-48-3

PREFACE

Since I began practising as a solicitor in 2005, I have been struck by the reputation TUPE has garnered as a particularly challenging area of employment law. The introduction of TUPE 2006 shortly afterwards, which revamped the previous regime that had existed since 1981, gave me an early opportunity to get stuck into the detail. I have been fascinated ever since.

This book is for lawyers in private practice, in-house counsel, HR practitioners and anyone else who may encounter TUPE as part of their work. I have aimed to explain the core legal principles, approach some of the complex areas in a straightforward way and offer my own perspective on how TUPE issues are managed on the ground, in day-to-day practice.

For a publication of this size, it has been necessary to avoid delving into the intricacies of every nuance in the case law. There are other excellent textbooks by eminent employment lawyers which already do this very comprehensively and with admirable aplomb. I do not seek to tread the same path.

TUPE presents ample opportunity for academic debate and the gleeful exploration of theoretical rabbit-holes. I have sought to resist such temptations and, where the law is grey or in a state of flux, tried to identify a sensible path through any complexity. Where recent developments have made this difficult (for example, following the decisions on fragmentation in *Govaerts* and *McTear* or the UK's post-Brexit legal landscape), I have called out the uncertainties as best I can.

Above all, my primary objective has been to produce something for a relatively wide audience that is concise, accessible and user-friendly. I will leave readers to judge whether that has been achieved.

I must include a few caveats and disclaimers. This book represents my own views and not those of my firm or anyone associated with it. It is not intended as a substitute for seeking legal advice on any particular set of circumstances – and should not be relied on as such. To my knowledge, the legal principles outlined in this book are correct as at 30 January 2023. Any errors or omissions are mine alone.

During my legal career to date, I have been very fortunate to work with (and against!) some exceptionally talented people who have helped me to refine my knowledge and hone my skills in advising and negotiating on TUPE matters. I have attended many seminars (more recently, webinars), read countless articles and textbooks and learned so much from the expertise of others. There are too many to mention individually but I am grateful to them all.

I would like to extend particular thanks to James Murray of Mishcon de Reya (who has been kind enough to review the draft and provide some much-needed constructive feedback) and Tim Kevan and Garry Wright at Law Brief Publishing (for approaching me about this project and providing guidance on my first foray into book writing).

Finally, a big thank you to my family, without whose support I would not have been able to sustain this undertaking (no pun intended), alongside my other commitments. They have done a sterling job in pretending to be as enthused by this subject as I am.

Dominic Holmes
January 2023

NOTE ON KEY TERMS AND SOURCE MATERIAL

In this book, I will use the following terms and abbreviations for ease of reference:

- "TUPE" means the Transfer of Undertakings (Protection of Employment) Regulations 2006 (as amended in 2014). On occasion, I will distinguish between these regulations and their predecessor by referring to "TUPE 1981" and "TUPE 2006".

- "ARD" means the Acquired Rights Directive. This is the primary EU legislation from which TUPE is derived.

- Unless otherwise specified, references to specific regulations relate to the legislative provisions of TUPE.

- TUPE applies to two distinct types of transfer. I will adopt the terminology "transfer of an economic entity" to refer to a transfer under Regulation 3(1)(a) and "service provision change" (or "SPC") to refer to a transfer under Regulation 3(1)(b).

- In terms of other UK legislation, "ERA" means the Employment Rights Act 1996 and "TULR(C)A" means the Trade Union and Labour Relations (Consolidation) Act 1992.

- You will see abbreviated references in the text and case references to various courts and tribunals. For those unfamiliar with the English court system, the first port of call for most employment claims (including those under TUPE) is the Employment Tribunal (or "ET"). Appeals from the ET go to the Employment Appeal Tribunal ("EAT"), then to the Court of Appeal ("CA") and finally to the UK Supreme Court ("UKSC"). The UKSC replaced the House of Lords ("HL") as the final domestic appellate court in 2009.

- Domestic courts in EU member states may request rulings on the interpretation of the ARD from the Court of Justice of the European Union ("CJEU"). Previously, they went to the European Court of Justice ("ECJ"), although technically the ECJ is simply one of the component parts of the CJEU.

- "BIS Guide" means the Department of Business Innovation and Skills' guidance on *"Employment Rights on the Transfer of an Undertaking"* dated January 2014.

As a general approach, it is always best practice to look at the primary source material first (namely, the relevant legislative provisions). This is an approach that will be adopted throughout.

I have also referred extensively to relevant case law – a necessity, given the extensive intervention by domestic and European courts in interpreting the requirements of TUPE and the ARD. For consistency, I have used the case citation from the Industrial Relations Law Reports (IRLR) where possible. However, most of the domestic judgments I have cited can be accessed freely online – for example, on the BAILII website. European case law authorities are available on EUR-Lex.

TABLE OF CASES

Abellio London Ltd v. Musse and ors [2012] IRLR 360 (EAT)

Abler v Sodexho MM Catering GmbH C-340/01, [2004] IRLR 168 (ECJ)

Adult Learning Inspectorate v Beloff (UKEAT/0238/07) (EAT)

Albron Catering BV v. FNV Bondgenoten and Roest C-242/09, [2011] IRLR 76 (ECJ)

Alemo-Herron and ors v Parkwood Leisure Ltd [2011] IRLR 696 (UKSC); C-426/11, [2014] IRLR 744 (CJEU)

Allen and ors v. Amalgamated Construction Co Ltd [2000] IRLR 119 (ECJ)*Amatori and ors v. Telecom Italia SpA and anor* C-458/12 [2014] IRLR 400 (ECJ)

Amicus and anor v. City Building (Glasgow) LLP and ors [2009] IRLR 253 (EAT)

Asklepios Kliniken Langen-Seiligenstadt GmbH v. Felja [C-680 & 81/15, [2017] IRLR 653 (CJEU)

Aspden v. Webbs Poultry and Meat Group (Holdings) Ltd [1996] IRLR 521 (QB)

Baker v. British Gas Services (Commercial) Ltd and anor [2017] EWHC 2302 (QBD)

Beckmann v Dynamco Whichloe Macfarlane Ltd C-164/00, [2002] IRLR 578 (ECJ)

Bernadone v. Pall Mall Services Group and ors [2000] IRLR 487 (CA)

Berriman v. Delabole Slate Ltd [1985] IRLR 305 (CA)

Betts v. Brintel Helicopters Ltd and anor [1997] IRLR 361 (CA)

Born London Ltd v. Spire Production Services Ltd [2017] IRLR 493 (EAT)

Botzen and ors v. Rotterdamsche Droogdok Maatshappij BV C-186/83, [1985] ECR 519 (ECJ)

Braganza v. BP Shipping Ltd [2015] ICR 449 (UKSC)

British Fuels Ltd v. Baxendale and anor; Wilson and ors v. St Helen's Borough Council [1998] IRLR 706 (HL)

BT Managed Services Ltd v. Edwards and anor [2015] IRLR 994 (EAT)

Cable Realisations Ltd v. GMB Northern [2010] IRLR 42 (EAT)

Capita Health Solutions v. McLean [2008] IRLR 595 (EAT)

Celtec Ltd v. Astley C-478/03, [2005] IRLR 647 (ECJ)

Cetinsoy and ors v. London United Busways UKEAT/0042/14 (EAT)

Chapman and anor v. CPS Computer Systems plc [1987] IRLR 462 (CA)

Cheesman and others v. R. Brewer Contracts Ltd [2001] IRLR 144 (EAT)

Clearsprings Management Ltd v. Ankers and anor UKEAT/0054/08 (EAT)

Collino and Chiappero v. Telecom Italia SpA C-343/98, [2000] IRLR 788 (ECJ)

Commerzbank AG v. Keen [2007] ICR 623 (CA)

Credit Suisse First Boston (Europe) Ltd v. Lister [1998] IRLR 700 (CA)

Department for Education v. Huke and anor UKEAT/0800/12 (EAT)

Dewhurst and ors v. Revisecatch Ltd (t/a Ecourier) and anor (Case number 2201909/2018) (ET)

DJM International Ltd v. Nicholas [1996] IRLR 76 (EAT)

Duncan Webb Offset (Maidstone) Ltd v. Cooper [1995] IRLR 184 (EAT)

Duncombe and ors v. Secretary of State for Children, Schools and Families [2011] IRLR 840 (UKSC)

Eddie Stobart Ltd v. Moreman and ors [2012] IRLR 356 (EAT)

Enterprise Management Services Ltd v. Connect-Up Ltd and ors [2012] IRLR 190 (EAT)

Fairhurst Ward Abbotts Ltd v. Botes Building Ltd and ors [2004] IRLR 304 (CA)

Federación de Servicios Públicos de la UGT v. Ayunamiento de la Línea de la Concepción and ors C-151/09, [2010] ICR 1248 (ECJ)

Ferguson and ors v. Astrea Asset Management Ltd [2020] IRLR 577 (EAT)

Foreningen af Arbejdslere i Danmark v. Daddy's Dance Hall A/S C-324/86, [1988] IRLR 315 (ECJ)

Grafe and Pohle v. Südbrandenburger Nahverkehrs GmbH C-298/18, [2020] IRLR 399

Green v. Elan Care Ltd UKEAT/18/01 (EAT)

Hare Wines Ltd v. Kaur and anor [2019] IRLR 555 (CA)

Hassard v. McGrath [1996] NI 586 (NICA)

Hazel and anor v. The Manchester College [2014] IRLR 392 (CA)

Henke v Gemeinder Schierke and Verwaltungsgemeinschaft "Brocken" C-298/94, [1996] IRLR 701 (ECJ)

Holis Metal Industries Ltd v. GMB and anor [2008] IRLR 187 (EAT)

Horizon Security Services Ltd v. Ndeze and anor [2014] IRLR 854 (EAT)

Hynd v. Armstrong [2007] IRLR 338 (CSIH)

Ibex Trading Co. Ltd (in administration) v. Walton and ors [1994] IRLR 564 (EAT)

ICAP Management Services Ltd v. Berry and anor [2017] IRLR 811 (QBD)

Inex Home Improvements Ltd v. Hodgkins [2016] IRLR 13 (EAT)

Institution of Professional Civil Servants v Secretary of State for Defence [1987] IRLR 373 (Ch)

ISS Facility Services NV v. Govaerts and anor C-344/18, [2020] IRLR 639 (CJEU)

Jackson Lloyd Ltd and anor v. Smith and ors UKEAT/0127/13 (EAT)

Jinks v. London Borough of Havering UKEAT/0157/14/MC (EAT)

Johnson Controls Ltd v. Campbell and anor UKEAT/0041/12 (EAT)

Kavanagh and ors v. Crystal Palace FC and anor [2014] IRLR 139 (CA)

Key2Law (Surrey) LLP v. De'Antiquis and anor [2011] IRLR 272 (CA)

Kimberley Group Housing Ltd v. Hambley and ors [2008] IRLR 682 (EAT)

Klarenberg v. Ferrotron Technologies GmbH C-466/07, [2009] IRLR 301 (ECJ)

Landsorganisationen i Danmark v. Ny Mølle Kro C-287/86, [1989] IRLR 37

Law Society of England and Wales v. Secretary of State for Justice and anor [2010] IRLR 407 (QBD)

Liddell's Coaches v. Cook and ors [2013] ICR 547 (EAT)

Litster v. Forth Dry Dock & Engineering Co Ltd [1989] IRLR 161 (HL)

LLDY Alexandra Ltd (formerly Loch Lomond Distillery Company Ltd) v. UNITE the Union and anor UKEATS/0002/14 (EAT)

London Metropolitan University v. Sackur and ors UKEAT/0286/06 (EAT)

Marshall v. Game Retail Ltd UKEAT/0276/12 (EAT)

Martin and ors v. South Bank University C-4/01, [2004] IRLR 74 (ECJ)

Mayeur v Association Promotion de L'Information Messine C-175/99, [2000] IRLR 783 (ECJ)

McCarrick v. Hunter [2013] IRLR 26 (CA)

McTear Contracts Ltd v. Bennett and ors [2021] IRLR 444 (EAT)

Micklefield v. SAC Technology Ltd [1990] IRLR 218 (Ch)

Millam v. The Print Factory (London) 1991 Ltd [2007] IRLR 526 (CA)

Mitie Managed Services Ltd v. French and ors [2002] IRLR 521 (EAT)

Morris Angel & Son Ltd v. Hollande and anor [1993] IRLR 169 (CA)

Nationwide Building Society v. Benn and ors [2010] IRLR 922 (EAT)

New ISG Ltd v. Vernon [2008] IRLR 45 (Ch)

Nicholls & anor v. London Borough of Croydon and ors [2018] IRLR 988 (EAT)

Nottinghamshire Healthcare and NHS Trust v. Hamshaw and ors UKEAT/0037/11 (EAT)

Oakland v. Wellswood (Yorkshire) Ltd [2010] IRLR 82 (CA)

OCS Group UK Ltd v. Jones and anor UKEAT/0038.09 (EAT)

Ottimo Property Services Ltd v. Duncan [2015] IRLR 806 (EAT)

Oy Liikenne AB v. Lisojärvi and Juntunen C-172/99, [2001] IRLR 171 (ECJ)

P14 Medical Ltd v. Mahon [2021] IRLR 39 (QB)

Pannu and ors v. Geo W King Ltd (in liquidation) and ors [2012] IRLR 195 (EAT)

PatSystems Holdings Ltd v. Neilly [2012] IRLR 979 (QB)

P.Bork International A/S (in liquidation) v. Foreningen af Arbejdsledere i Danmark C-101/87, [1989] IRLR 41 (ECJ)

Ponticelli (UK) Ltd v. Gallagher [2022] EAT 140 (EAT)

Pressure Coolers Ltd v. Molloy and ors [2011] IRLR 630 (EAT)

QLog Ltd v. O'Brien and ors UKEAT/0301/13/JOJ (EAT)

Rask and anor v. ISS Kantineservice A/S C-209/21, [1993] IRLR 133 (ECJ)

Ravat v. Halliburton Manufacturing and Services Ltd [2012] IRLR 315 (UKSC)

RCO Support Services Ltd v. Unison [2002] IRLR 401 (CA)

Regent Security Services Ltd v. Power [2008] IRLR 66 (CA)

Rynda (UK) Ltd v. Rhijnsburger [2015] IRLR 394 (CA)

Scattolon v. Ministero dell'Istruzione, dell'Universita et della Ricerca C-108/10, [2011] IRLR 1020 (ECJ)

Schmidt v. Spar und Leihkasse der Frühren Ämter Bordesholm, Kiel und Croshagen [1994] IRLR 302 (ECJ)

Seawell Ltd v. Ceva Freight (UK) Ltd and anor [2012] IRLR 802 (EAT)

Serco Ltd v. Lawson [2006] IRLR 289 (HL)

Smith and ors v. Trustees of Brooklands College UKEAT/028/11 (EAT)

SNR Denton LLP v. Kirwan and anor [2012] IRLR 966 (EAT)

Solectron Scotland Ltd v. Roper and ors [2004] IRLR 4 (EAT)

Spaceright Europe Ltd v. Baillavoine [2012] IRLR 111 (CA)

Spijkers v. Gebroeders Benedik Abbatoir C-24/85, [1986] CMLR 296 (ECJ)

Susie Radin v. GMB and ors [2004] IRLR 400 (CA)

Süzen v. Zehnacker Gebäudereinigung GmbH Krankenhausservice C-13/95, [1997] IRLR 255 (ECJ)

Sweetin v. Coral Racing [2006] IRLR 252 (EAT)

Tapere v South London and Maudsley NHS Trust [2009] IRLR 972 (EAT)

The Proctor & Gamble Company and ors v. Svenska Cellulosa Aktiebolaget SCA and anor [2012] IRLR 733 (Ch)

The Salvation Army Trustee Company v. Bahi and ors [2017] IRLR 410 (EAT)

Thompson v. SCS Consulting Ltd and ors [2001] IRLR 801 (EAT)

Todd v. Strain and ors [2011] IRLR 11 (EAT)

Tuitt v. London Borough of Richmond-upon-Thames [2022] EAT 124 (EAT)

UNISON v. Somerset County Council and ors [2010] IRLR 207 (EAT)

University of Oxford v. Humphreys [2000] IRLR 183 (CA)

Werhof v. Freeway Traffic Systems GmbH & Co. KG C-499/04, [2006] IRLR 400 (ECJ)

Whent and ors v. T Cartledge Ltd [1997] IRLR 153 (EAT)

Xerox Business Services Philippines Inc Ltd v. Zeb [2018] IRLR 495

CONTENTS

CHAPTER ONE

TUPE: INTRODUCTION AND OVERVIEW

For more than 40 years TUPE has proved to be one of the trickiest areas of employment law in the UK. It has been fertile ground for employment lawyers advising organisations on the potential transfer (or non-transfer) of staff in the context of business sales, public sector transfers, commercial services and insolvencies.

Origins

TUPE is derived from European legislation that was first introduced in 1977. Specifically, it comes from, EC Council Directive 77/187 *"on the approximation of the laws of Member States relating to the safeguarding of employees' rights in the event of transfers of undertakings, businesses or parts of businesses"*. This is quite a mouthful, so it is more commonly known as the "Acquired Rights Directive". Many practitioners simply refer to it as the "ARD".

In common with all EC (now EU) Directives, member states were obliged to introduce local implementing legislation to transpose the minimum requirements of the ARD into national law, within a given timeframe. This was done by the UK Parliament through the Transfer of Undertakings (Protection of Employment) Regulations 1981.

Fast forward 17 years and the EU Council adopted a revised Directive (98/50/EC). This sat alongside the original 1977 Directive, until they were consolidated by a revamped Acquired Rights Directive (2001/23/EC).

This was implemented in the UK by the current legislation, the Transfer of Undertakings (Protection of Employment) Regulations 2006. TUPE 2006 incorporated the amendments required by the new ARD, including rules relating to insolvent businesses and imposing joint and several liability on the transferor and transferee for failure to inform and consult.

Of course, the ARD has been interpreted and implemented in different ways by the UK and each of the (now 27) EU member states, to reflect their varying domestic employment law landscapes, politics, industrial relations practices and work cultures. This has resulted in quite significant differences in the approaches to, for example, how pensions are treated or the processes for informing and consulting with employee representatives.

The UK has had a somewhat chequered history with the ARD. The UK Governments of the 1980s and 1990s had a less than enthusiastic approach to it, to the extent that TUPE 1981 was found to be non-compliant in failing to respect the minimum safeguards set out in the ARD.

However, as we shall see, arguably it has done a complete about-turn with TUPE 2006 and not only embraced, but significantly "gold-plated", the minimum ARD protections by introducing a new concept of "service provision change". As far as I am aware, this legislative approach is unique to the UK and has not been followed elsewhere.

TUPE 2006 also introduced, for the first time, an obligation on the transferor to provide minimum employee liability information to the transferee at least 14 days before the transfer. In 2014, this was extended to 28 days. Again, this requirement is not mandated in the ARD and many EU member states do not have similar provisions.

Following Brexit, at the time of writing the ARD remains part of "retained EU law" under the European Union (Withdrawal) Act 2018. This means that TUPE (consistent with other domestic legislation derived from EU law) continues to be interpreted by reference to

European case law up to 31 December 2020. As I explain in the epilogue to this book, this could change quite radically in the future.

The absolute basics: when TUPE applies and what that means

Despite its reputation for labyrinthine complexity, TUPE is a relatively short and straightforward piece of legislation. Difficulties arise in practice, largely because its application is often fact-sensitive and/or it has potentially unwanted commercial consequences for one or more of the parties involved. This has not been helped by a string of confusing court decisions (both at domestic and EU level), which have caused uncertainty in how TUPE should be interpreted.

However, the core legal principles are easily understood. As a very high-level overview:

1. TUPE will apply either where there is: (a) a transfer of an economic entity that retains its identity (typically, where there is the sale of all or part of a business or its assets); or (b) a change in who performs activities or services on behalf of a customer. These concepts are not mutually exclusive – some scenarios may constitute both a transfer of an economic entity (in the traditional ARD sense) and a service provision change.

2. In the public sector, certain types of administrative reorganisations and transfers of administrative functions fall outside TUPE. However, the Secretary of State can make an order that TUPE protections will apply in specific cases (and has done so in the past). Failing that, there is a Cabinet Office Statement of Practice which stipulates that TUPE principles should be followed, if TUPE does not otherwise apply.

3. If TUPE does apply:

    a. An employee who is assigned to the transferring economic entity or services (commonly known as an "in-scope employee") will automatically become employed by the transferee on their existing terms and conditions of employment, unless they object to the transfer. The effect of TUPE is to novate their contract of employment to the transferee.

b. The transferee will inherit most pre-transfer rights and liabilities relating to the transferring employees (with some exceptions). They will effectively step into the shoes of the outgoing employer, with effect from the transfer date.

c. Unless there is an economic, technical or organisational reason entailing changes in the workforce (known commonly as an "ETO reason"), dismissals made because of the transfer will be automatically unfair. This will be the case regardless of whether dismissal occurs pre- or post-transfer. Employees can also resign and claim unfair dismissal if substantial changes are proposed to their terms and conditions to their material detriment. Unfair dismissal protection is only available to employees with at least two years' continuous service.

d. Similarly, with some exceptions, changes to terms and conditions made by the transferee because of the TUPE transfer will be void, unless there is an ETO reason.

Parts A and B of this book consider each of the above in more detail.

Complex legal issues

Although the core principles are easy to follow, there are undoubtedly areas of complexity, or instances where the law is difficult to apply in practice.

In **Part C**, I will look at the law and practice relating to the following questions:

1. Fragmentation: To whom does an in-scope employee transfer, if either: (a) an economic entity (or part of an economic entity) is transferred from one transferor to multiple transferees; or (b) services are re-tendered or outsourced to multiple new service providers?

2. Trade unions and collective agreements: To what extent does a collective agreement survive a TUPE transfer and continue to bind the transferee? When can the transferee depart from collective terms agreed pre-transfer? Does it have to recognise unions who represent transferring employees?

3. Pensions: What are the transferee's obligations in relation to the pension rights of transferring employees?

4. TUPE and insolvency: What happens if the transferor becomes insolvent, but some or all of its business or assets are sold to help pay creditors?

5. Bonuses, benefits and share schemes: How does a transferee replicate any bonus or share-based incentives for which a transferring employee would have been eligible with their previous employer? What are the transferee's obligations in relation to benefits and perks it may inherit, given that some of these may be non-contractual and the transferee may have its own benefits arrangements or third party providers in place?

6. Restrictive covenants: To what extent can a transferee rely on post-termination restrictions it inherits (such as obligations not

to compete, solicit customers or staff or interfere with supplier relationships), which have been entered into between a transferring employee and the transferor? Can the transferee introduce new restrictive covenants?

TUPE processes

In **Part D**, I look at the relevant processes that result from a TUPE transfer.

In particular, a transferor is required to provide certain "employee liability information" to the transferee regarding in-scope employees.

There is also a duty on both employers to inform (and, in certain circumstances, consult with) representatives of affected employees, in good time before the transfer takes place. The category of "affected employees" will often extend beyond those who are simply in scope to transfer.

TUPE in practice

Finally, in **Part E**, I will share some experience of how TUPE actually operates in the real world – and how the parties can deal effectively with the myriad of commercial issues that arise.

I will look at negotiating indemnities which seek to apportion employment costs between parties (and circumvent the default position that most liability transfers to the transferee) and other provisions that might be prudent to include (or exclude) from a commercial agreement.

I will cover the practical considerations that arise from TUPE, from the perspective of each of the outgoing employer (transferor), incoming employer (transferee) and, in the case of re-tendering services, the customer who will be one step removed from any movement of staff. I will explore effective strategies for managing TUPE projects, from initial preparation to post-transfer integration.

I will also look at TUPE in the context of transfers into or out of the UK – and how employers might approach cross-border or multi-jurisdictional transactions.

But first things first. Let's begin by exploring what a TUPE transfer actually is.

PART A

DOES TUPE APPLY?

CHAPTER TWO

TRANSFER OF AN ECONOMIC ENTITY

The first of the two types of "relevant transfer" governed by TUPE is that for which the ARD was originally introduced – and which has formed the basis for transfer of undertakings legislation across the EU for over 40 years.

I will call this the "transfer of an economic entity", to distinguish it from the more recent UK-specific statutory concept of "service provision change"[1].

Key principles

Regulation 3(1)(a) states that TUPE applies to:

> *"a transfer of an undertaking, business or part of an undertaking or business situated immediately before the transfer in the United Kingdom to another person where there is a transfer of an economic entity which retains its identity."*

We must look at the constituent elements of that definition in turn, to determine whether TUPE applies in any given scenario. There are five questions to consider:

1. Is there an economic entity?

2. Does the economic entity transfer to another person?

---

[1] See **Chapter 3**

3. Does the economic entity retain its identity in the hands of the transferee?
4. Is the economic entity situated in the UK immediately before the transfer?
5. When does the transfer take place?

Economic entity

Regulation 3(2) provides a simple definition of "economic entity" as follows:

> *"an organised grouping of resources which has the objective of pursuing an economic activity, whether or not that activity is central or ancillary"*

This wording mirrors precisely the definition in Article 1(1)(b) of the ARD.

It should be contrasted with the concept of an "organised grouping of <u>employees</u>", which is used in the context of service provision changes. The distinction is deliberate, and its importance will become apparent.

Further, Regulation 3(4)(a) confirms that TUPE applies to:

> *"public and private undertakings engaged in economic activities whether or not they are operating for gain"*

The scope is wide and it will usually be easy to satisfy this element of the test.

It will cover publicly and privately-owned commercial enterprises of all sizes (regardless of the corporate, partnership or other vehicle that is used), from multi-national plcs with thousands of staff across multiple sites to an individual who employs a single employee in their personal capacity. It can include the NHS, government departments and public sector bodies, educational establishments, temp agencies, charities and not-for-profit organisations.

Any organisation that carries out any type of economic activity will potentially count as an economic entity, even if that activity is not the main purpose of the organisation and regardless of whether it is intended to be profit-making. This means a support function within a larger business (such as marketing, IT or facilities management) can constitute its own economic entity, even though the principal objective of the undertaking as a whole is focused elsewhere.

However, the economic entity must have at least some structure and autonomy, even if it does not have significant assets. This is an important principle.

As we shall see, the approach to determining whether the entity "retains its identity" will differ, depending on how it is found to be constituted in the first place. An "asset heavy" entity which does not transfer any significant assets is unlikely to fall within TUPE, whereas this criterion is much less relevant for "labour intensive" entities, which essentially comprise one or more people doing work with few assets.

In this way, we can see that a cleaning business employing one individual (the frequently cited person with a mop and bucket[2]) can be just as much an "economic entity" as a large manufacturing business with factory premises, machinery, stock, goodwill and intellectual property rights in the design of its products. The underlying purpose of TUPE and the ARD to safeguard employee rights is paramount, regardless of the size of the employer or the number of employees potentially affected.

A useful summary of the case law and relevant principles can be found in EAT's decision in *Cheesman and others v. R. Brewer Contracts*

---

2 See, for example, *Schmidt v. Spar und Leihkasse der Frühren Ämter Bordesholm, Kiel und Croshagen* [1994] IRLR 302 (ECJ)

Limited[3]. Although decided over 20 years ago in the context of TUPE 1981, the landscape in relation to the transfer of an economic entity (and whether it retains its identity) has not changed significantly. *Cheesman* is one of the leading domestic authorities in this area.

As Regulation 3(1)(a) confirms, there can also be a transfer of part of an undertaking.

This occurred in *Fairhurst Ward Abbotts Ltd v. Botes Building Ltd and ors*[4], where a maintenance contract was re-tendered by a local council and split into two separate lots based on geography, with each lot awarded to a different bidder. The Court of Appeal held that TUPE applied in this case. Even though resources were not organised by geography pre-transfer:

> *"it is sufficient if a part of the larger stable economic entity becomes identified for the first time as a separate economic entity on the occasion of the transfer separating a part from the whole."*[5]

Of course, each case is fact-specific and the decision may have been different if the contract had been split up in a different way, or dissipated across a larger number of new providers.

Fairhurst is arguably inconsistent with the subsequent ECJ decision in *Amatori and ors v. Telecom Italia SpA and anor*[6], which stated that the ARD would not apply if the entity did not have *"sufficient functional autonomy"* before the transfer (although this did not preclude Member States from legislating otherwise).

---

3 [2001] IRLR 144 (EAT), paragraph 10. It has since been approved by the Court of Appeal in *McCarrick v. Hunter* [2013] IRLR 26 (CA).

4 [2004] IRLR 304 (CA)

5 *Fairhurst*, paragraph 32

6 C-458/12, [2014] IRLR 400 (ECJ)

This issue of fragmentation has also become more complicated following the recent CJEU decision in *ISS Facility Services NV v. Govaerts and anor*[7], to which we return in **Chapter 10**.

Even if there is an economic entity, the question of whether it retains its identity must still be determined. However, the fact that it may subsequently not remain a distinct entity post-transfer (for example, where it is absorbed into the transferee's wider operations) does not preclude TUPE from applying[8].

Transfer to another person

In the very first operative provision of the ARD, Article 1(1)(a) states:

> *"This Directive shall apply to any transfer of an undertaking business, or part of an undertaking of business to another employer as a result of a legal transfer or merger."* (emphasis added).

The reference to a *"legal transfer or merger"* is vague – but perhaps necessarily so, as it needs to cater for different types of transaction under the domestic laws of each EU Member State.

However, the ARD is very clear that a transfer must involve a change of employer. In similar terms, TUPE refers to *"a transfer... to another person"*[9].

European case law has repeatedly and consistently addressed this point. The clearest exposition is in *Landsorganisationen i Danmark v. Ny Mølle Krø*[10]:

---

7 C-344/18, [2020] IRLR 639 (CJEU)

8 *Klarenberg v. Ferrotron Technologies GmbH* C-466/07, [2009] IRLR 301 (ECJ)

9 Regulation 3(1)(a)

10 C-287/86, [1989] IRLR 37, paragraph 12

> *"The Directive is therefore applicable where, following a legal transfer or merger, there is a change in the legal or natural person who is responsible for carrying on the business and who by virtue of that fact incurs the obligations of an employer vis-à-vis employees of the undertaking."*

TUPE can apply to transfers between two businesses that are entirely unrelated or to an intra-group transfer between two associated companies, with a common ultimate parent. It is prudent to consider whether a simple proposal to move employees to a different entity within the same corporate group might trigger a TUPE transfer, therefore requiring more than a simple letter to employees confirming the change of employer.

As a general principle, the purchase of some or all of the share capital in a company will not trigger a TUPE transfer. Although the ownership of the employing entity may change, the employer itself remains the same.

There is, of course, scope for an exception – for example, where the purchaser assumes de facto control of the employment-related activities previously done by the employer (such as paying staff and managing pensions). The most commonly cited example of this is *Millam v. The Print Factory (London) 1991 Limited*[11], where the integration of the target company's business into that of the purchaser was deemed to fall within TUPE[12].

Such cases are likely to be quite rare in practice. Compare *Millam* to the subsequent High Court decision in *ICAP Management Services Limited v. Berry and anor*[13], where a share transaction did not result in a TUPE transfer.

---

11 [2007] IRLR 526 (CA)

12 See also *Jackson Lloyd Ltd and anor v. Smith and ors* UKEAT/0127/13 (EAT)

13 [2017] IRLR 811 (QBD)

A separate decision to move assets or employees in the context of a wider share transaction may still fall within TUPE, even if it does not happen immediately pre- or post-acquisition. This could happen, for example, where staff are moved by the seller into a "Newco" (which is the target company of the share transaction) or where the buyer decides to hive across the target company's assets to another group entity, as part of an internal reorganisation.

Retaining identity

For TUPE to apply to the transfer of an economic entity, Regulation 3(1)(a) stipulates that it must "retain its identity" in the hands of the transferee. But what does this mean in practice?

The leading ECJ authority is *Spijkers v. Gebroeders Benedik Abbatoir*[14]. The *Spijkers* "multi-factoral test" has withstood the passage of time for over 35 years and remains the first point of reference for practitioners advising clients on the application of TUPE. It is worth citing in full:

> *"12. ...a transfer of an undertaking, business or part of a business does not occur merely because its assets are disposed of. Instead it is necessary to consider, in a case such as the present, whether the business was disposed of as a going concern, as would be indicated, inter alia, by the fact that its operation was actually continued or resumed by the new employer, with the same or similar activities.*
>
> *13. In order to determine whether those conditions are met, it is necessary to consider all the facts characterizing the transaction in question, including the type of undertaking or business, whether or not the business's tangible assets, such as buildings and movable property, are transferred, the value of its intangible assets at the time of the transfer, whether or not the majority of its employees are taken over by the new employer, whether or not its customers are transferred and the degree of similarity between the activities carried on before*

[14] C-24/85, [1986] CMLR 296 (ECJ)

> *and after the transfer and the period if any for which those activities are suspended. It should be noted, however, that all those circumstances are merely single factors in the overall assessment which must be made and cannot therefore be considered in isolation."*

There has been a substantial body of European and domestic case law since *Spijkers* which has had to grapple with applying these principles to a multitude of factual scenarios.

It is a highly fact-sensitive exercise, and an exhaustive analysis of these judgments is beyond the scope of this book. Different parties to a transaction will inevitably emphasise or downplay certain factors to suit their own narrative, depending on whether they want a transfer to occur.

For this reason, it is easy to see why determining whether there has been a transfer of an economic entity is one of the most mercurial aspects of TUPE. Save in the most clear-cut of situations, it can be difficult to advise on this issue with complete certainty.

However, there are some guiding principles which provide the outlines of a clear path through what can seem a confusing morass:

1. <u>Don't stray too far from *Spijkers*</u>

   The courts have stressed time and again that the *Spijkers* test is the only one that really matters. All relevant *Spijkers* factors should be considered in any particular set of circumstances and given appropriate weight, according to the context.

   Outside of this, attempts to equate any given factual matrix with a case authority decided on what are perceived to be analogous facts can often be unhelpful.

2. Establish the type of entity

The weight to be attached to each element of the *Spijkers* test will differ, depending on the activity carried on[15] – hence the importance of establishing what the economic entity is, in the first place.

A distinction has evolved between the approaches to "asset heavy" entities (where the relevant economic activity requires the use of significant tangible or intangible assets) and "labour intensive" entities (which require people to do the work but perhaps not much else). Manufacturing would typically be "asset heavy" whereas certain types of professional services would not.

3. Asset heavy undertakings: Consider what assets will actually be used?

Where the assets are owned by the transferor and not sold or transferred to the transferee, this does not necessarily preclude a TUPE transfer[16]. However, it is more difficult in such cases to demonstrate that the undertaking has retained its identity.

If the assets used by the transferor are owned by a third-party customer and are then subsequently made available to and used by the transferee, there can still be a TUPE transfer[17]. But these are not hard and fast rules.

To illustrate where the boundary sits, a useful comparison can be made between two European authorities concerning the

---

[15] See *Süzen v. Zehnacker Gebäudereinigung GmbH Krankenhausservice* C-13/95, [1997] IRLR 255 (ECJ)

[16] *Cheesman*, paragraph 11(vii), citing *Allen and ors v. Amalgamated Construction Co Ltd* [2000] IRLR 119 (ECJ), paragraph 30

[17] See for example, *Abler v Sodexho MM Catering GmbH* C-340/01, [2004] IRLR 168 (ECJ)

transfer of public bus services to a new provider. In both cases, the principal tangible assets required to deliver the services (that is, the buses) were not transferred – but there were different outcomes.

In *Oy Liikenne AB v. Lisojärvi and Juntunen*[18], the transfer of seven local bus routes in Helsinki fell outside the scope of the ARD. Although most of the employees were taken on by the new provider, the buses were not. It leased two buses from the old provider for a few months (pending the delivery of 22 new buses) and purchased some driver uniforms, but that was it. The ECJ concluded that:

> *"in a sector such as scheduled public transport by bus, where the tangible assets contribute significantly to the performance of the activity, the absence of a transfer to a significant extent from the old to the new contractor of such assets, which are necessary for the proper functioning of the entity, must lead to the conclusion that the entity does not retain its identity."*[19]

Conversely, in *Grafe and Pohle v. Südbrandenburger Nahverkehrs GmbH*[20], the CJEU ruled that there was a transfer of an undertaking. The tender process required that buses should not exceed a certain age and had to comply with a given environmental standard (which the existing provider's buses did not). Accordingly, the assets could not have been used by the successful bidder in any event and the decision not to take them on did not prevent the ARD from applying.

This factual nuance allowed the CJEU to distinguish this case from the approach taken in *Oy Liikenne*. Potentially good news for the two claimant bus drivers (both of whom had over 35 years' continuous service, before being dismissed by the

18 C-172/99, [2001] IRLR 171 (ECJ)

19 *Oy Liikenne*, paragraph 42

20 C-298/18, [2020] IRLR 399

outgoing provider) – although the matter was sent back to the referring German court for final determination.

4. Labour intensive undertakings: It's not all about the people

Regulation 3(6)(b) states that a transfer may take place whether nor not any property is transferred to the transferee by the transferor. This simply confirms the position in *Spijkers* and subsequent case law, namely that the absence of a transfer of assets will not be determinative of itself.

Where there are no significant tangible or intangible assets involved in performing the activity that constitutes the "economic entity", the retention of its identity cannot logically depend on the transfer of such assets[21]. Therefore, the other factors identified in *Spijkers* will assume greater weight. Specifically, in *Süzen*, the ECJ ruled:

> *"it must be recognized that such a [labour intensive] entity is capable of maintaining its identity after it has been transferred where the new employer does not merely pursue the activity in question but also takes over a major part, in terms of their numbers and skills, of the employees specifically assigned by his predecessor to that task."*[22]

This principle has been applied by our domestic appellate courts (including the Court of Appeal) in several subsequent cases[23].

On its face, it appears to give significant control to the transferee in determining whether or not TUPE applies, assuming that: (a) there is not otherwise a "service provision

---

[21] *Cheesman*, paragraph 11(vi), citing (amongst others) *Allen*, paragraph 28

[22] *Süzen*, paragraph 21

[23] See, for example, *Betts v. Brintel Helicopters* Ltd *and anor* [1997] IRLR 361 (CA)

change" transfer (see **Chapter 3**); and (b) the transferor does not choose to redeploy its employees pre-transfer.

For example, the transferee can choose not to employ existing staff, but take on new staff on such terms (and in such numbers) as it wishes, with the transferor footing the bill for any redundancy costs. Or it can inherit the current staff and utilise their experience in performing the activities in question, albeit constrained by the fact that their existing terms and continued employment will be protected by TUPE.

However, in practice, this should be approached with care. The judicial treatment of *Süzen* in the UK suggests that the importance of a transferee's decision not to take on staff should not be overstated. For example, in *RCO Support Services Ltd v. Unison*[24], the Court of Appeal ruled that the transfer of a labour-intensive entity may still fall within TUPE even where the major part of the workforce (in terms of numbers and skills) is not taken on, especially if other *Spijkers* factors (such as the transfer of customers and similarity of activities) are in play.

It might be argued that a conscious decision to avoid TUPE applying by not taking on staff might, in fact, have the opposite effect. However, as always, there is a danger of being distracted from the multi-factoral *Spijkers* test which, although not exhaustive, makes no reference to deliberate avoidance measures.

Commercially, the transferee's choice may be dictated by customer preference, if it is participating in a tender process to take on services. This will, no doubt, be factored into the overall cost of those services. In that regard, the terms of any existing contract between the customer and an incumbent service provider may give a putative transferee access to employee

[24] [2002] IRLR 401 (CA)

information, to enable it to assess what it might inherit before making its decision and bidding accordingly.

Situated in the UK

Although the economic entity must be situated in the UK, it is possible that some or all of the employees who are in scope to transfer are based overseas. Under Regulation 3(4)(c), TUPE can apply to:

> *"a transfer of an undertaking, business or part of an undertaking or business (which may also be a service provision change) where persons employed in the undertaking business or part transferred ordinarily work outside the United Kingdom."*

The approach in any given case will depend on the type of undertaking.

For an "asset heavy" entity, the focus will be on the location of the relevant tangible and intangible assets. It is these which will comprise the economic entity and, therefore, determine where it is situated immediately before the transfer. A manufacturer selling its UK-based factory, equipment and stock will likely fall within TUPE, even if there are regional sales employees in other countries.

There will be some areas of uncertainty. For example, assets may be scattered across jurisdictions – perhaps dotted across Europe to support an increasingly remote or mobile workforce, working from home or on the road. Physical assets may be in the UK but intellectual property rights may be registered elsewhere – so it may be necessary to assess the relative importance of the proportion of tangible assets against the value of the underlying intellectual property rights, to identify the relevant undertaking.

For a "labour intensive" entity, the location of the employees will be more important. If a major part of the workforce (in terms of numbers or skills) is based in the UK, TUPE is more likely to apply.

In both cases, if the "economic entity" is in the UK, the transfer may have an impact on employees in other countries. I will return in **Chapter 19** to look more broadly at the impact of cross-border transfers – including the circumstances in which an employee assigned to a transferring economic entity but based outside the UK might be able to claim rights under TUPE.

Finally, it is worth noting that the considerations which apply to a service provision change transfer are different. The relevant test in those circumstances is that there must be an *"organised grouping of employees situated in Great Britain"*[25]. It is an important distinction, particularly if a transfer could potentially comprise both the transfer of an economic entity (under Regulation 3(1)(a)) and a service provision change (under Regulation 3(1)(b)).

Timing of the transfer

In many cases, it will be self-evident when the transfer takes place.

For a business sale, it is likely that the economic entity will transfer on the date the relevant assets are sold to the transferee.

Similarly, if the transfer relates to re-tendered services, it will usually be the date on which the incumbent provider ceases operations and the new provider takes over.

Sometimes, to provide certainty, an asset purchase agreement (or contract for services) will stipulate the precise "effective time" of transfer – for example, 00.01 on the completion date (or services commencement date). This will be helpful in the vast majority of cases, but not conclusive.

There may be circumstances where the position is less clear-cut. For example, the assets comprising the economic entity may be passed to the buyer gradually, or through a succession of transactions. This might

[25] Regulation 3(3)(a)(i)

potentially result in two (or more) separate TUPE transfers, if each part that is transferred can be considered a stable economic entity in its own right.

If not, Regulation 3(6)(a) ensures that the parties cannot circumvent TUPE by a "drip-feed" of assets or employees, by confirming that a relevant transfer *"may be effected by a series of two or more separate transactions"*. The question of precisely when the contracts of employment transfer is one of fact.

When appointing a new service provider, there may be a long transition period. There may even be a separate transition services agreement, detailing how the existing activities will be phased out and ensuring a smooth handover as the new services are ramped up. This raises an important question – can there be a gradual transfer of employees over a period of time?

The emphatic answer is no. In *Celtec Ltd v. Astley*[26], the ECJ stated that the transfer date is:

> *"the date on which responsibility as employer for carrying on the business of the unit transferred moves from the transferor to the transferee. That date is a particular point in time which cannot be postponed to another date at the will of the transferor or transferee."*

Just as the parties cannot bypass TUPE by agreeing whether it applies, they cannot engineer when it applies. If we return to the statutory wording, we need to consider at what point the relevant undertaking *"retains its identity"* in the hands of the transferee.

For an asset-heavy entity, it will likely be when most of the core assets required to carry out the relevant activity are transferred. Without these, it is difficult to see how the transferee can become responsible for carrying on the business of the unit transferred (as outlined in *Celtec*).

---

[26] C-478/03, [2005] IRLR 647 (ECJ)

For a labour-intensive undertaking, it may be when a substantial proportion of the employees (in terms of numbers or skills) begin working for the new employer (and effectively drag the others who are assigned to the work over with them). Again, without the employees to do the work in an otherwise asset-light business, the transferee may not be able to carry out the relevant activity that is being transferred.

However, these issues need to be considered in their full context. A protracted delay in the principal assets or employees coming across might ultimately be relevant in whether the economic entity retains its identity at all. A temporary cessation of activities will not, in itself, prevent TUPE from applying[27]. However, if activities are suspended altogether for a lengthy period and the post-transfer activities look quite different when resumed, any delay may carry greater weight.

Let's use a practical example to illustrate this. An Italian restaurant of 15 years' standing is sold to a new owner and then closed for refurbishment. The employees are made redundant by the seller. The buyer takes on vacant possession, but the sale includes kitchen equipment.

The buyer rips out the kitchen and undertakes a major refit and rebranding exercise. The restaurant re-opens for business four months later as a café bar, specialising in cocktails and Spanish tapas. In those circumstances, it is hard to see how TUPE might apply. Some assets have come across, but several have not – the seller has taken away the tables, chairs and other assets required for serving food and drink to guests. The activities have been put on hold for an extended period and when they resume, there is little similarity with what went on before.

Compare this to a different scenario where the buyer redecorates front-of-house, but re-opens as an Italian restaurant with the same name, telephone number and website, a couple of weeks later. This is much more likely to fall within TUPE – there is value in the intangible assets

[27] *P.Bork International A/S (in liquidation) v. Foreningen af Arbejdsledere i Danmark* C-101/87, [1989] IRLR 41 (ECJ)

(which will likely attract back loyal customers of the old business), the suspension of activities has been limited and the undertaking remains similar when it re-opens. It has, quite clearly, retained its identity, albeit under new ownership.

As the case law demonstrates, there are several other ways in which the facts in this simple example can be altered, to illustrate the various shades of grey. It neatly encapsulates the interplay of factors that will be relevant to whether there is a transfer of an economic entity under Regulation 3(1)(a). As ever, the correct analysis starts and ends with *Spijkers*.

CHAPTER THREE

SERVICE PROVISION CHANGES

Since 2006, TUPE has expressly recognised a second, separate type of "relevant transfer". This occurs where a customer appoints or changes a service provider, or brings services that are carried out by a third party back in-house. These are known collectively as "service provision changes" or "SPCs".

The purpose of creating a new statutory concept of "SPC" was to circumvent the potential uncertainty caused by applying the test for a "transfer of an economic entity" in such circumstances. It is generally viewed as a "gold-plating" of the minimum requirements of the ARD. It is not an approach that has been adopted elsewhere in the EU.

The criteria for an SPC are different to those for the transfer of an economic entity. As such, a parallel but distinct body of case law from our domestic courts has evolved, largely free from the influence of CJEU jurisprudence[1].

The overall effect of judicial interpretation in this area has been to define quite narrowly the circumstances in which an SPC is deemed to apply. Where the SPC test is not met, the same set of facts may still give rise to a transfer of an economic entity, under Regulation 3(1)(a) (see **Chapter 2**).

---

1 Although there have been occasions where European case law has been leant upon to support analysis of the SPC regime – for example, in *Inex Home Improvements Ltd v. Hodgkins* [2016] IRLR 13 (EAT)

Key principles

Regulation 3(1)(b) states that TUPE applies to:

> *"a service provision change, that is a situation in which:*
>
> *(i) activities cease to be carried out by a person ('a client') on his own behalf and are carried out instead by another person on the client's behalf ('a contractor');*
>
> *(ii) activities cease to be carried out by a contractor on a client's behalf (whether or not those activities had previously been carried out by the client on his own behalf) and are carried out instead by another person ('a subsequent contractor') on the client's behalf; or*
>
> *(iii) activities cease to be carried out by a contractor or a subsequent contractor on a client's behalf (whether or not those activities had previously been carried out by the client on his own behalf) and are carried out instead by the client on his own behalf"*

In summary, TUPE may apply where there is an **outsourcing**, a **change in contractor** (also known as a "second generation outsourcing") or an **insourcing** of services.

Regulation 3(1)(b) is subject to various other conditions being satisfied. There are five questions to consider:

1. Who are the relevant parties involved?

2. After the transfer, will the activities be fundamentally the same as before?

3. Is there an organised grouping of employees which has as its principal purpose the carrying out of those activities?

4. Is the organised grouping of employees based in Great Britain?

5. Does the client intend that the activities will be carried out by the transferee on an ongoing basis – that is, other than in connection with a single specific event or task of short-term duration?

Clients and contractors

Regulation 3(1)(b) envisages up to three parties being involved in an SPC – the "client", the "contractor" and (for second generation outsourcings only) the "subsequent contractor".

Although it will often be self-evident, identifying these parties is a necessary first step in analysing whether there is an SPC at all. It is not always as straightforward as it seems.

The "client" is the entity which contracts with a third party for the services (or brings them in-house, having previously outsourced them). This may be different to the individuals who ultimately benefit from the activities (such as the end-users of public services funded and contracted out by a local council).

The identity of the "client' must remain the same[2]. Therefore, for example, if the owner of a shopping centre sells the building and the buyer appoints a different property management company to run the site, there will be no SPC. Both the client and contractor will have changed.

An SPC can occur where there is a group of clients that are sufficiently linked, so that they have a common intention for the activities to be carried out by the transferee (in accordance with Regulation 3(3)(a)(ii)). However, the group must remain the same after the relevant activities have passed to a new provider[3]. If services are insourced by a group of

2 *McCarrick v. Hunter* [2013] IRLR 26 (CA)

3 *Ottimo Property Services Ltd v. Duncan* [2015] IRLR 806 (EAT)

clients, there may be potential fragmentation issues to consider. This is considered in **Chapter 10**.

Complications can arise where services are sub-contracted (or proposed to be sub-contracted). I consider this in more detail in **Chapter 5**.

"Fundamentally the same" activities

Regulation 3(2A) states that the activities to be carried out by the transferee must be *"fundamentally the same"* as those previously carried out by person who has ceased to do them (the transferor).

This requirement was introduced in 2014 and effectively codified the case law interpretation of the SPC rules up to that point.

It requires a careful identification of the type and nature of: (a) the existing activities that are being carried out; and (b) the replacement activities to be performed by someone else. As ever, it is a question of fact and the judicial guidance suggests that the approach taken should be neither too generalised nor too pedantic[4].

In practice, this question is often the main area of focus, where parties disagree as to whether there is an SPC. For example, a client may wish to appoint a new contractor or bring activities in-house because the quality of existing service delivery is poor or because the work can be done more efficiently (perhaps in the way it is organised or in the use of technology). In those cases, it will not likely want employees to transfer automatically. For similar reasons, the new contractor may deliberately design the replacement services to be different.

Conversely, the existing contractor may have no other work for the employees to do. It will seek to argue that the new activities <u>are</u> fundamentally the same, to avoid having to carry out redundancies itself (and absorb the associated costs).

---

4 See, for example, *The Salvation Army Trustee Company v. Bahi and ors* [2017] IRLR 410 (EAT)

The statutory language is more restrictive than that used to identify a transfer of an economic entity, under the *Spijkers* test. This requires an assessment of "*the degree of similarity between the activities carried on before and after the transfer*", but does not stipulate that they must be "*fundamentally the same*". Further, similarity of activities it is only one of several factors to be considered under *Spijkers*, whereas a finding that new services are not "*fundamentally the same*" is, of itself, fatal to an SPC.

Sometimes, it will be easily apparent that the new activities are quite different to what has gone on before. However, there have been instances where even apparently minor changes to the type of activity or the ways in which they have been carried out have meant that TUPE does not apply.

There are several useful case examples to draw on. The EAT has held that there was no SPC where:

- a hot food catering service at a work canteen was replaced by sandwich and salad bar[5];
- nursing services provided to residents at a care home were replaced by carers visiting residents in their individual homes[6];
- a centralised taxi booking co-ordinator was replaced by secretaries ordering taxis directly from a cab firm[7];
- there was a substantial change in the amount of technical IT support required by a local council, when it brought services in-house[8];

5 *OCS Group UK Ltd v. Jones and anor* UKEAT/0038.09 (EAT)

6 *Nottinghamshire Healthcare and NHS Trust v. Hamshaw and ors* UKEAT/0037/11 (EAT)

7 *Johnson Controls Ltd v. Campbell and anor* UKEAT/0041/12 (EAT)

8 *Department for Education v. Huke and anor* UKEAT/0800/12 (EAT)

- IT services to schools were re-tendered and the new services only omitted 15% of the work which had comprised the previous services. This was considered sufficiently different, even without fragmentation of the services to six new providers[9]; and

- dedicated CCTV monitoring services were brought in-house by a local council and performed by existing staff alongside other duties, thus reducing the level of monitoring that took place[10].

A different approach was taken in *The Salvation Army Trustee Company v. Bahi and ors*[11], where a local council re-tendered accommodation support services for homeless individuals. Those service users had previously been dispersed across ten houses with multiple occupants. The contract was awarded to The Salvation Army, which provided accommodation in two large hostels. There were various other differences, such as the age range of those covered, the maximum duration they could stay in supported accommodation and the provision of a 24-hour concierge service on-site (rather than the mere availability of 24-hour support if needed).

The EAT determined in *Bahi* that an employment tribunal had been entitled to conclude that activities <u>were</u> fundamentally the same, under Regulation 3(2A). This may seem a slightly surprising outcome, given the preceding case law. However, if the employment tribunal had determined that the activities were not fundamentally the same, it seems likely that the EAT would have upheld that decision too. It was a judgement call on the facts.

---

9 *Enterprise Management Services Ltd v. Connect-Up Ltd and ors* [2012] IRLR 190 (EAT)

10 *Tuitt v. London Borough of Richmond-upon-Thames* [2022] EAT 124 (EAT)

11 [2017] IRLR 410 (EAT)

Finally, TUPE will not apply if the activities *"consist wholly or mainly of the supply of goods for the client's use"*[12]. As is self-evident from the term "service provision change", we are concerned with services. Where contracts involve a mixture of goods and services, the exclusion will only apply if the activities consist *"mainly"* of the supply of goods[13].

Organised grouping of employees

Regulation 3(3)(a)(i) requires that, immediately before the service provision change:

> *"there is an organised grouping of employees situated in Great Britain which has as its principal purpose the carrying out of the activities concerned on behalf of the client."*

Where the activities are performed by or on behalf of Client A, the transferor (whether that is Client A itself or an external service provider) must have an identifiable "Client A team" that is specifically tasked with doing that particular work for Client A.

In *Eddie Stobart Ltd v. Moreman and ors*[14], a group of employees employed in a warehouse facility packed and processed meat exclusively for one customer (Vion). However, this was due to the shift system that was in operation. Vion placed its orders at a particular time of day, meaning that the same employees serviced their requirements each day. There was no conscious decision by Eddie Stobart to create a "Vion team" and, therefore, no organised grouping of employees.

---

12 Regulation 3(3)(b)

13 An example of this is *Pannu and ors v. Geo W King Ltd (in liquidation) and ors* [2012] IRLR 195 (EAT)

14 [2012] IRLR 356 (EAT)

In *Rynda (UK) Ltd v. Rhijnsburger*[15], the Court of Appeal expanded on the EAT's reasoning in *Eddie Stobart* and outlined a four-stage test focused on the outgoing employer ("company B"):

> *"The first stage of this exercise is to identify the service which company B was providing to the client. The next step is to list the activities which the staff of company B performed in order to provide that service. The third step is to identify the employee or employees of company B who ordinarily carried out those activities. The fourth step is to consider whether company B organised that employee or those employees into a 'grouping' for the principal purpose of carrying out the listed activities."*[16]

Both limbs of the test must be satisfied – "organised grouping" and "principal purpose".

Rynda is an example where there was an organised grouping of employees comprising a single person[17] (in this case, a commercial property manager). He was deliberately designated to perform work for a specific client and therefore the necessary principal purpose was established too.

Conversely, in *Seawell Ltd v. Ceva Freight (UK) Ltd and anor*[18], a single individual who worked exclusively for one client (as part of a team servicing multiple clients) did not trigger an SPC. There was no deliberate decision to organise the activities so that he spent 100% of his time on one client, so he could not constitute an "organised grouping of employees" on his own. The EAT was clear that this could not be *"a matter of happenstance"*[19]. Similarly, although he was a member of a bigger team of eight employees, that team worked for

15 [2015] IRLR 394 (CA)

16 *Rynda*, paragraph 44

17 This is expressly envisaged in Regulation 2(1)

18 [2012] IRLR 802 (EAT)

19 *Seawell*, paragraph 17

several clients and therefore did not have as its "principal purpose" the performing of activities for his specific client.

If an organised grouping of employees has been established, the question of which employees are "assigned" to it (under Regulation 4(1)) is distinct and must be considered separately.[20]

Situated in Great Britain

Regulation 3(3)(a)(i) requires that, immediately before the service provision change, the organised grouping of employees must be *"situated in Great Britain"*.

There are two important differences between this test and the corresponding territoriality rules relating to the traditional transfer of an economic entity (which are considered in **Chapter 2**).

First, SPCs deal with an *"organised grouping of employees"*, not an *"organised grouping of resources"*. For the transfer of an economic entity, there is more scope for employees based abroad to be caught by TUPE, if the assets or other relevant constituent parts of the economic entity are in the UK. For SPCs, there is greater emphasis on where the employees who actually do the work are physically based.

There is surprisingly little guidance on this important issue, given the proliferation of multi-jurisdictional teams and remote working in recent years. The BIS Guide gives the example of a website maintenance contract being re-tendered and suggests that if one of the IT technicians works outside Great Britain, that should not prevent TUPE applying. However, if the whole team worked from abroad, there would be no SPC[21].

---

[20] See **Chapter 6**

[21] BIS Guide, page 14. See **Chapter 19** for a detailed discussion on managing international transfers in practice.

It would seem likely from this that the greater the proportion of employees in the "client team" that are based outside Great Britain, the less likely it is that TUPE would apply in the SPC context. At the very least, a substantial majority of the staff comprising the "client team" would need to be situated in Great Britain. There is nothing to suggest that the ECJ's *Süzen* test[22] (looking at a major part of the workforce *"in terms of their numbers and skills"*) would be considered relevant. For SPCs, the probable focus is on pure numbers, rather than a qualitative assessment of each individual's skills or importance to the services.

Secondly, the relevant territory for SPCs is Great Britain, not the United Kingdom. This means that, unlike a transfer of an economic entity, Regulation 3(1)(b) does not apply to Northern Ireland.

There is corresponding separate legislation in Northern Ireland which introduces the concept of SPCs in the same way (and applies to an organised grouping of employees in Northern Ireland only)[23]. However, there may be a scenario where services provided to a client from both Northern Ireland and Great Britain do not constitute an SPC, because there is no distinct "organised grouping of employees" in one or both jurisdictions.

Single specific event or task of short-term duration

Regulation 3(3)(a)(ii) requires that, immediately before the service provision change:

> *"the client intends that the activities will, following the service provision change, be carried out by the transferee other than in*

---

22 *Süzen v. Zehnacker Gebäudereinigung GmbH Krankenhausservice* C-13/95, [1997] IRLR 255 (ECJ) – see **Chapter 2** for a detailed consideration of *Süzen* and related case law

23 The Service Provision Change (Protection of Employment) Regulations (Northern Ireland) 2006. An analysis of these regulations (and any difference in approach to the rest of the UK) is outside the scope of this book.

> *connection with a single specific event or task of short-term duration."*

This wording has given rise to some confusion. Does a *"single specific event"* need to be *"of short-term duration"*, or does that requirement only apply to a *"task"*? If a single specific event of any duration is excluded, it could potentially remove protection from employees assigned to work on long-term projects.

This was addressed in *SNR Denton LLP v. Kirwan and anor*[24], where the EAT considered that "short-term duration" applied to both tasks and single specific events. The opposite view was taken by a differently constituted EAT shortly afterwards, in *Liddell's Coaches v. Cook and ors*[25].

The point has yet to be resolved satisfactorily, but the approach in *Kirwan* would seem more in keeping with the broad purpose of the legislation. It is also consistent with the BIS Guide, which envisaged that the provision of security advice to the organisers of an Olympic Games for a period of several years before the event could be caught by the SPC regime (whereas security arrangements for athletes during the Games would not)[26].

More generally, *Kirwan* provides useful guidance on the interpretation of other aspects of Regulation 3(3)(a)(ii). The primary focus should be on what the client intended, at the time the SPC is said to have taken place.

Further, what the client considers or intends to be "short-term duration" at that juncture is (somewhat predictably) *"a matter of fact and degree"*[27]. In *Liddell's Coaches*, for example, a contract to transport children to school for a period of one year was deemed short-term,

---

24 [2012] IRLR 966 (EAT), paragraph 41

25 [2013] ICR 547 (EAT), paragraphs 29 and 30

26 BIS Guide, page 11

27 *Kirwan*, paragraph 44

because typically such transport services contracts lasted for three to five years. The one-year contract was specifically intended by the local authority to cover a temporary need to ferry pupils to a different site, whilst their school was being rebuilt.

CHAPTER FOUR

PUBLIC SECTOR TRANSFERS

TUPE is widely defined to apply to *"public and private undertakings engaged in economic activities, whether or not they are operating for gain"*.

This will ordinarily include transfers into and out of the public sector, and transfers between public sector organisations, provided that the relevant public undertaking is engaged in economic activities (which, as we have seen, is a relatively low bar).

There are two specific additional considerations when dealing with the public sector.

First, the Cabinet Office Statement of Practice on Staff Transfers in the Public Sector[1] (or "**COSOP**") widens the protection of employees in certain transfer scenarios which would otherwise fall outside TUPE.

Secondly, in contrast, there is a specific exception in Regulation 3(5), which brings certain types of internal public sector reorganisation outside of TUPE altogether.

COSOP

COSOP sets out an expectation that TUPE principles should be followed for certain types of public sector transfer, regardless of whether the strict requirements for a transfer of an economic entity or a service provision change are actually met.

---

1 January 2000 (revised December 2013)

Although it is not legally binding, COSOP provides a clear framework that *"the Government expects all public sector organisations to work within"*[2]. In particular:

- transfers *"will be conducted on the basis that staff will transfer and TUPE should apply, unless there are genuinely exceptional reasons not to do so"*;
- where TUPE does not apply in strict legal terms, the principles of TUPE should be followed and affected staff should be treated no less favourably than had TUPE applied; and
- there should be *"appropriate arrangements to protect occupational pensions, redundancy and severance terms"* (including Fair Deal pension arrangements).[3]

These principles will apply to the following types of public sector transfer:

- unless there are genuinely exceptional reasons[4]:
    - o the transfer of staff from the public sector to a private sector employer or voluntary sector body, as a result of a Public Private Partnership[5];
    - o second and subsequent transfers, where staff originally transferred from the public sector and the relevant public contracting authority re-tenders those services[6];

---

[2] COSOP, paragraph 1

[3] COSOP, paragraph 5

[4] COSOP, paragraphs 14 to 16 set out guidance on exceptions

[5] COSOP, paragraphs 10 to 11

[6] COSOP, paragraph 12

- o the transfer of services back into the public sector, where staff originally transferred from the public sector[7];

- transfers and reorganisations within the public sector including, for example, transfers involving local government, Civil Service Departments and Agencies, non-departmental government bodies (or "NDPBs") and the NHS[8]; and

- transfers and reorganisations within the Civil Service[9].

The public sector exception

Notwithstanding the wide application of COSOP, there is an overarching exception within TUPE, relating to internal public sector reorganisations. Regulation 3(5) states:

> *"an administrative reorganisation of public administrative authorities or the transfer of administrative functions between public administrative authorities is not a relevant transfer."* [10]

In these circumstances, TUPE does not apply, even if the relevant arrangements would otherwise have constituted the transfer of an economic entity or a service provision change. I will call this the "public sector exception".

Neither *"administrative functions"* nor *"public administrative authorities"* are defined in the legislation. Further, there is limited guidance from the domestic or European courts on these principles.

---

7 COSOP, paragraph 13

8 COSOP, paragraphs 17 to 20

9 COSOP, paragraphs 21 to 22

10 This wording mirrors the corresponding provision in Article 1(1)(c) of the ARD

The public sector exception initially developed from the ECJ's decision in *Henke v Gemeinder Schierke and Verwaltungsgemeinschaft "Brocken"*[11]. This case concerned the secretary to a local mayor's office, whose employment was terminated when administrative functions relating to the mayor's municipality were combined with those in other municipalities. The ECJ held that there was no transfer and she was not protected from dismissal.

Subsequently, the ECJ confirmed in *Mayeur v Association Promotion de L'Information Messine*[12] that *"only the reorganisation of structures of the public administration or the transfer of administrative functions between public administrative authorities are excluded"*[13].

Notably, the Advocate General in *Mayeur* opined that the principle in *Henke* only covered posts which involve *"a genuine participation, directly or indirectly, in the exercise of public authority and in the functions intended to safeguard the general interests of the State or other public bodies"*[14]. He gave, as examples, roles in national defence, internal security, public finances, the judicial system and home affairs and posts in ministries and central banks, provided that the activities are centred on a political or judicial power.

This is illustrated by *Scattolon v. Ministero dell'Istruzione, dell'Universita et della Ricerca*[15], where the public sector exception did not apply to the transfer of cleaning, maintenance and administrative assistance services in state-run schools. These activities were of an economic nature and did not fall within the exercise of public powers.

In the UK, the courts have held that a *"public administrative authority"* included (and Regulation 3(5) applied to) for example, the Adult

[11] C-298/94, [1996] IRLR 701 (ECJ)

[12] C-175/99, [2000] IRLR 783 (ECJ)

[13] *Mayeur*, paragraph 33

[14] Opinion of AG Lèger in *Mayeur* (13 June 2000), paragraph 61

[15] C-108/10, [2011] IRLR 1020 (ECJ)

Learning Inspectorate[16] (an NDPB body carrying out inspection work in respect of further education and vocational and work-based training, which became part of Ofsted) and the Law Society's Legal Complaints Service[17] (a private sector organisation which provided redress to the public by adjudicating on complaints about poor quality professional legal services, whose functions were transferred to a new Office for Legal Complaints).

More recently, the scope of Regulation 3(5) has been given detailed judicial consideration in *Nicholls & anor v. London Borough of Croydon and ors*[18]. The EAT drew a clear distinction between: (a) exercising *"public powers" or 'public authority"*; and (b) carrying on *"economic activities"*. They are mutually exclusive concepts – the former will fall outside TUPE, the latter within[19].

COSOP suggests that Regulation 3(5) applies to *"only a relatively limited range of situations involving the transfer of entities pursuing non-economic objectives within the public sector"* whilst acknowledging that it has still to be tested fully by the courts[20]. However, this conclusion should be treated with caution. The current version of COSOP is dated December 2013 and predates *Nicholls,* where the EAT considered it was not helpful to see Regulation 3(5) as an exception which is to be strictly construed, although it *"must be kept within its proper bounds"*.

This indicates a more open-minded approach although, in practice, COSOP principles may well be followed regardless of Regulation 3(5). Failing that, the Secretary of State has the statutory power to introduce regulations making "TUPE-like provision" to cover specific transfer

---

16 *Adult Learning Inspectorate v Beloff* (UKEAT/0238/07) (EAT)

17 *Law Society of England and Wales v. Secretary of State for Justice and anor* [2010] IRLR 407 (QBD)

18 [2018] IRLR 988 (EAT)

19 See *Nicholls*, paragraphs 45 to 55

20 COSOP, paragraph 18

scenarios[21] that fall outside TUPE (and has done so on previous occasions).

[21] s.38 Employment Relations Act 1999

CHAPTER FIVE

SUB-CONTRACTORS

When providing commercial services, a service provider may nominate one or more sub-contractors to perform some or all of the relevant activities to its client. This may be because it does not have the specialist expertise to carry out elements of the work itself, or simply because it does not have the resources to satisfy the totality of the client's requirements.

For example, a client may own or lease large commercial premises and contract out a broad range of facilities management services to a centralised provider (such as cleaning, security, maintenance or reception desk duties). The provider will then bring in third party sub-contractors in as necessary, to perform some or all of these tasks, whilst remaining directly accountable to the client for the quality of the services.

In another scenario, an IT services provider may need to bring in expertise from a specialist individual consultant, who may contract with the provider on an individual basis or through a personal services company or umbrella arrangement.

This can cause complications when the customer decides to replace the service provider or bring the work in-house. The sub-contractor will usually have no direct contract relationship with the end-client and the employees who actually do the work may not be employed by the service provider (or an employing entity within its own corporate group).

This issue comes up frequently in practice and is not always straightforward.

Key principles

Regulation 2(1) states that:

> *"references to 'contractor' in regulation 3 shall include a sub-contractor".*

The easiest way to visualise this is simply to substitute the word "contractor" for "sub-contractor" when considering the relevant SPC scenario in Regulation 3(1)(b). The EAT has summarised it neatly as follows, in the context of an in-sourcing:

> *"Regulation 3(1)(b)(iii) can be satisfied where '(iii) activities cease to be carried out by a [sub-contractor]... on a client's behalf... and are carried out instead by the client on his own behalf...'"*[1]

This seems clear enough. However, it does not always sit easily with the principle established in *McCarrick v. Hunter*[2] that, for there to be an SPC, the identity of the client must not change.

Using the example above, before the activities cease to be carried out, the sub-contractor's "client" is arguably the principal contractor (which, in turn, contracts with the end-client). After the end-client terminates the services provided by the principal contractor and brings the work in-house, the "client" carrying out those activities will be the end-client, not the principal contractor.

The key question is, where a sub-contractor carries out work *"on a client's behalf"* under Regulation 3(1)(b), whether before or after the putative transfer, who is the real "client" for those purposes?

There have been some reported cases involving sub-contractor relationships, which have approached them in different ways. For practical purposes, it is useful to consider three separate scenarios, namely where:

---

1 *Jinks v. London Borough of Havering* UKEAT/0157/14/MC (EAT)

2 [2013] IRLR 26 (CA)

- an outgoing sub-contractor is replaced by either: (a) a new principal contractor providing services directly to the client; or (b) the client itself (where activities are taken in-house);
- an incoming sub-contractor is appointed by a new principal contractor, where activities were previously performed directly by either: (a) the outgoing contractor; or (b) the client itself; and
- activities move from one sub-contractor to another.

Outgoing sub-contractors

In *Horizon Security Services Ltd v. Ndeze and anor*[3], a local council owned a business centre. It was managed through a separate entity (Workspace) which, in turn, sub-contracted on-site security services to PCS. Mr Ndeze was employed by PCS as a security guard who was dedicated to working at the business centre.

The council ended its contract with Workspace. Following this, the council contracted directly with Horizon to provide security services (PCS had also bid unsuccessfully for the work). Mr Ndeze was dismissed by PCS and the question arose as to whether liability for that dismissal transferred to Horizon.

The EAT held that there was no TUPE transfer as the identity of the client had changed. PCS's client had been Workplace (the intermediary property management company), whereas Horizon's client was the council. In its judgment:

> *"the assessment of who is the client in a service provision change case will generally be a matter for the Employment Tribunal as a finding of fact... Regulation 3(1)(b) plainly recognises subcontractor cases and the possibility of a service provision change in such circumstances*

3 [2014] IRLR 854 (EAT)

> *is thus envisaged under (iii). That, however, is about the change in provider; it does not define the client."*[4]

A similar question came before the EAT shortly afterwards. In *Jinks v. London Borough of Havering*[5], a local council owned a site comprising an ice-skating rink and a car park. It contracted with Saturn Leisure to provide property management services. Saturn Leisure sub-contracted car park management services to Regal, which employed Mr Jinks. The council terminated its contract with Saturn Leisure, closed the ice rink and subsequently managed the car park itself.

Based on the principles in *McCarrick v. Hunter*, the Employment Tribunal had struck out Mr Jinks' claim that liability for his dismissal had transferred under TUPE from Regal to the council. It considered that Regal's client had been Saturn Leisure, not the council which had subsequently brought the activities in-house. The EAT overturned this decision, ruling that:

> *"the Employment Judge took an impermissible shortcut by treating the client of a sub-contractor as necessarily being, and only being, the contractor to which it was contractually bound to provide a service... The Horizon case supports the conclusion that the strict legal contractual relationships do not necessarily answer the Regulation 3 question."*[6]

On that basis, the case was remitted back to the Tribunal to consider whether, additionally or alternatively to Saturn, the council could be viewed as Regal's real client.

In my view, there is scope to distinguish the facts in *Jinks* from those in *Horizon*, such that a SPC could be found to have occurred in *Jinks*.

---

4 *Horizon*, paragraphs 46 to 47

5 UKEAT/0157/14/MC (EAT)

6 *Jinks*, paragraph 24

When looking at whether services are provided *"on the client's behalf"*, it seemed relevant in *Horizon* that the council merely owned the building. Workspace rented out the office spaces within the business centre to its own clients and during office hours, the security guard would assist visitors and take telephone calls on behalf of Workspace and its clients (not the council).

Query whether the outcome may have been different, if the council had offered office space directly to local businesses, who paid the council directly for using those facilities. In those circumstances, it might have been open to the Tribunal to conclude that PCS was performing activities on the council's behalf (even though contractually, Workspace was PCS's client).

In *Jinks*, when Regal managed the car park, it made the spaces available to local NHS staff by issuing permits (as well as to users of the ice rink). Unlike in *Horizon*, the ultimate beneficiaries of Regal's services were not the customers of the principal contractor (Saturn). After the contract with Saturn was terminated, the local council initially granted a licence to the NHS trust to use the car park for its staff but, after a few months, converted it into a public car park. Both NHS employees and the general public benefited from this service.

Incoming sub-contractors

In *QLog Ltd v. O'Brien and ors*[7], a manufacturer of cardboard packaging (Ribble) contracted with a haulage company (McCarthy) to distribute its products to its customers across the UK. Ribble terminated the contract with McCarthy and engaged QLog in its place. QLog was a logistics company which sub-contracted the haulier services to a number of third party providers, who bid for each delivery by providing a quote on QLog's software platform.

---

7 UKEAT/0301/13/JCJ (EAT)

The EAT held that there was no service provision change. However, it did not consider the sub-contractor argument at all. The case was decided on the basis that the services provided by QLog were not fundamentally the same as those previously provided by McCarthy (and therefore there was no transfer from McCarthy to QLog).

The question of a potential transfer from McCarthy to one or more of QLog's sub-contractors did not arise. Had the case been argued on that basis, the Employment Tribunal would have needed to consider whether the sub-contractors engaged by QLog performed services on Ribble's behalf, for the purposes of Regulation 3(1)(b)(ii). Adopting the logic used in *Horizon* and *Jinks* (which were decided shortly after *QLog*), it might reasonably have concluded that Ribble was the real client. After all, unlike in *Horizon*, the services were provided for the benefit of Ribble's customers, on Ribble's behalf.

This may seem like conjecture (as the point did not actually arise in *QLog*) but it is an important question. There will frequently be instances in practice where a new contractor sub-contracts services that were previously provided directly to the client by the outgoing contractor. It may be in the interests of the one or more parties to argue that some or all employees transfer to one or more sub-contractors.

In such cases, the sub-contractor issue is unlikely to be determinative in itself. Depending on the facts, it may be that there is no TUPE transfer, because the relevant sub-contractor only provides services in connection with a single specific event or task of short-term duration[8]. Taking the facts in *QLog*, each delivery could be deemed as a discrete, one-off assignment. However, some sub-contractors might get sufficiently regular work such that this exception does not apply.

Following the recent decisions in *Govaerts*[9] and *McTear*[10], it would also now be necessary to grapple with the difficult issue of fragmentation

---

8 Regulation 3(3)(a)(ii) – see **Chapter 3**

9 *ISS Security Services NV v. Govaerts and anor* C-344/18, [2020] IRLR 639 (CJEU)

(and the possibility that an employee might be employed by multiple sub-contractors, post-transfer). This is considered in more detail in **Chapter 10**.

As ever, the factual matrix is key, but it demonstrates the potentially tangled web which practitioners may need to unpick, where sub-contractors are introduced by a new provider.

Sub-contractor to sub-contractor

What happens where one sub-contractor is replaced by another?

Where the principal contractor maintains its relationship with the end-client, the analysis is likely to be straightforward. Essentially, it is a second generation outsourcing and the usual tests for determining whether there is an SPC will apply. Regardless of whether the principal contractor or the end-client is considered to be the "client" under Regulation 3(1)(b)(ii), the identity of the client will not change.

The position may be more complex where the end-client replaces an outgoing principal contractor with a new principal contractor, which in turn sub-contracts the relevant services. Should employees of a sub-contractor engaged by the outgoing principal contractor transfer to a different sub-contractor engaged by the new principal contractor? This question will be determined by reference to the (admittedly limited) guidance in *Horizon* and *Jinks*.

If there is a chain of sub-contractor relationships, such that the ultimate provider of the work is several steps removed from the relationship between principal contractor and end-client, this may weaken the argument that the activities are being done *"on behalf of"* that end-client. However, I am not aware of any judicial authority on this point.

---

[10] *McTear Contracts Ltd v. Bennett and ors* [2021] IRLR 444 (EAT)

In *Jinks*, for example, the focus was on a sub-contractor appointed by the principal contractor:

> *"If A contracts with B to provide it with a service, A is obviously the customer or client, If B then sub-contracts to C to provide part of that service, plainly B is, or at very least may be, the client or customer of C. But can A also be, by virtue of the sequence of transactions, a client of C in respect of the service it provides?"*[11]

The question of what would happen if C sub-contracted to D and so on, has yet to be considered.

Sub-contractors and Regulation 3(1)(a)

The analysis set out above only applies in the context of SPCs.

It may also be necessary to consider whether any of the scenarios we have considered above could amount to the transfer of an economic entity. In *McCarrick v. Hunter,* the Court of Appeal left open the possibility that even if the client changes, this may not preclude a TUPE transfer under Regulation 3(1)(a):

> *"It may be that where the business is in the nature of a service provided to a particular client, the identity of the client is an essential element in the description of the undertaking. If that is so, the services carried on for the new client would constitute a different undertaking and there would be no transfer. But that is an argument for another day."* [12]

That argument has yet to be played out. However, even if Regulation 3(1)(a) could potentially be invoked, any introduction, removal or change of sub-contractor relationship would still need to satisfy the *Spijkers* multi-factoral test. This is considered in detail in **Chapter 2.**

[11] *Jinks*, paragraph 22

[12] *McCarrick*, paragraph 48

PART B

BASIC PROTECTIONS

CHAPTER SIX

AUTOMATIC TRANSFER OF EMPLOYEES

Once it has been established that TUPE applies, the next question to consider is who transfers[1].

Identifying which individuals are "in scope" is important. They will be subject to the automatic transfer principle, have the right to participate (or elect a representative to participate) in the pre-transfer information and consultation process and be entitled to preserve their existing terms of employment. They may also have protection from unfair dismissal because of the transfer.

There is sometimes an arm-wrestle over who precisely should transfer. A transferor may want to retain valuable employees it has invested in and trained up (or it may want them to transfer, to avoid redundancy costs). A transferee may not be able to resource the activities properly without experienced and skilled employees following the work (or they may not need more staff at all). A customer who is changing providers will want some control, where the underlying motive is to ensure skills and knowledge are retained (or, conversely, to jettison employees who have delivered sub-standard service).

The employee who does not want to transfer always has the option to object and walk away, although this is relatively rare in practice[2]. The

1 Strictly speaking, TUPE does not talk about the transfer of employees, but their contracts are stated to have effect as if originally made with the transferee. It is, however, common parlance to talk about the transfer of employees.

2 An individual whose contract might otherwise have transferred under TUPE has the right to object to a transfer under Regulation 4(7). This exception is explored in **Chapter 8**.

transferor and transferee do not have that luxury. Just as they cannot bypass TUPE by agreeing between themselves whether (or not) TUPE applies, so they cannot agree to whom it applies.

Despite this, the parties to a commercial agreement will often try to establish some certainty by agreeing a schedule of employees who are intended to transfer. There may be an attempt to cherry-pick certain individuals, despite what TUPE says. Different commercial indemnities may apply to those on the list, compared to those who are not (but who subsequently claim that they should have been).

But how do we decide who goes across and who doesn't? And if we can't agree, where are the battlegrounds between the parties?

Key principles

Regulation 4(1) states:

> *"Except where objection is made under paragraph (7), a relevant transfer shall not operate so as to terminate the contract of any person employed by the transferor and assigned to the organised grouping of resources or employees that is subject to the relevant transfer, which would otherwise be terminated by the transfer, but any such contract shall have effect after the transfer as if originally made between the person so employed and the transferee."*

Regulation 4(3) states that this principle applies to:

> *"a person so employed immediately before the transfer or who would have been so employed if he had not been dismissed in the circumstances described in Regulation 7(1)..."*

To determine whether an individual is "in scope", we need to consider the following questions:

1. Is the individual an "employee"?

2. Are they employed by the transferor?

3. Are they assigned to the organised grouping of resources or employees?

4. Are they assigned immediately before the transfer?

Definition of "employee"

TUPE applies to an "employee", which is defined in Regulation 2(1) as:

> *"any individual who works for another person whether under a contract of service or apprenticeship or otherwise but does not include anyone who provides services under a contract for services."*

Compare this to the definition of "employee" under s.230(1) ERA 1996, which is confined to someone who works under a contract of employment (being a contract of service or apprenticeship).

The reference to *"or otherwise"* in Regulation 2(1) indicates that TUPE applies to a broader group of individuals than those who would be considered employees under ERA 1996. However, confusion arises because we do not know how much wider that category is. The inconsistency in defining "employee" across various pieces of legislation is unhelpful[3].

In particular, it is unclear whether the TUPE definition of "employee" will include individuals who would be classified as "limb (b) workers" under s.230(3)(b) ERA 1996. This includes anyone who works under *"any other contract... whereby the individual undertakes to do or perform*

[3] It is also different to the concept of "employment" under s.83(2) of the Equality Act 2010, which refers to *"employment under a contract of employment, a contract of apprenticeship or a contract personally to do work"*.

personally any work or services for another party to the contract whose status is not by virtue of the contract that of a client or customer of any profession or business undertaking carried on by the individual".

There are two possible interpretations of Regulation 2(1). It could exclude limb (b) workers, because TUPE does not apply to anyone providing services under a *"contract of services"*. However, if that is correct, what is meant by the reference to *"or otherwise"*? It is difficult to see how a further sub-category of individual unique to TUPE transfers, sitting somewhere between "employee" and "limb (b) worker", might be defined (and it would be highly undesirable).

Alternatively, it could be said that an "employee" for TUPE purposes includes limb (b) workers and the exclusion of those working under a *"contract of services"* simply refers to those who are genuinely in business on their own account. However, this does not answer satisfactorily the question of why limb (b) workers are not expressly included in the statutory drafting. Unlike s.230(3)(b) ERA 1996, there is no reference in Regulation 2(1) to the exclusion only applying to individuals who work for clients or customers of their own business.

So far, there has been no judicial assessment of this important question by the appellate courts. However, it has been considered by employment tribunals at first instance, most notably in *Dewhurst and ors v. Revisecatch Ltd (t/a Ecourier) and anor*[4].

In *Dewhurst*, the employment tribunal determined that limb (b) workers should be included in the Regulation 2(1) definition of "employee" (and are therefore covered by TUPE).

This decision was based on adopting a purposive interpretation of TUPE, in the wider context of the ARD. In particular, it noted that the underlying purpose of the legislation was to safeguard individual rights, in the event of a change of employer. It concluded that:

---

4 Case number 2201909/2018 (ET)

> *"Our 'general employment law' protects both limb b) workers and traditional employees, at different levels of protection, and both of these classes have their rights preserved by TUPE 2006."*

The exclusion of "contracts for services" in Regulation 2(1) was limited to *"independent contractors who are genuinely in business on their own account and do not have any employment / labour law rights to be preserved in the event of a transfer"*.

Although *Dewhurst* is only a first instance decision (and therefore not binding authority), it is a well-reasoned judgment. The safest approach is to assume that TUPE will apply to limb (b) workers, pending consideration of this issue by the EAT or above in a future case.

In practical terms, this results in a two-tier system. Limb (b) workers may be "employees" for TUPE purposes, but they are not "employees" under the ERA and therefore unable to claim unfair dismissal if their contract is terminated because of a TUPE transfer[5]. Their existing contractual terms will be protected in theory, although if the transferee does not like the terms it inherits, it can simply terminate the contract (without the risk of unfair dismissal liability). However, if it chooses to retain the individual and negotiate changes to the contract, these may be void and/or the individual may choose to cherry-pick which terms apply[6].

Employed by the transferor

Regulation 4(1) applies to employees of *"the transferor"*. In practice, the entity which is transferring all or part of an undertaking or ceasing activities as part of a service provision change may be different to the entity which employs the individuals to do the relevant work.

---

5 Issues relating to dismissals in the context of a TUPE transfer are considered in more detail in **Chapter 8**.

6 Issues relating to changes to terms and conditions are considered in more detail in **Chapter 9**.

For example, in corporate group structures, it is relatively common for individuals to be employed by a service company set up for that purpose, which is separate to the part of the business that is involved in the transfer. For international corporations, there may be a multi-jurisdictional transfer where the UK subsidiary employs the individuals but the relevant commercial transaction is entered into by an overseas parent company which owns the assets or has contracted to provide services.

As a basic principle, such arrangements should not preclude TUPE from applying.

This point was considered by the ECJ in *Albron Catering BV v. FNV Bondgenoten and Roest*[7], where an in-house catering function operated by Heineken was outsourced to a new provider (Albron) but the employees assigned to it were employed by a centralised employing entity within the Heineken group. The ECJ confirmed that the lack of a direct contractual relationship between the entity engaged in the relevant activities and the employees performing those activities did not bring them outside the ARD. It invoked the possibility of a "non-contractual employer" being identified as the transferor:

> *"the position of a contractual employer, who is not responsible for the economic activity of the economic entity transferred, cannot systematically take precedence, for the purposes of determining the identity of the transferor, over the position of a non-contractual employer who is responsible for that activity."*[8]

This case (and others in the domestic courts) have only dealt with this question in relation to the transfer of an economic entity. It remains to be seen whether a different approach might be taken in the context of service provision changes, given the narrow interpretation adopted by the courts to SPCs more generally[9]. In particular, Regulation 3(1)(b)

7 C-242/09, [2011] IRLR 76 (ECJ)

8 *Albron*, paragraph 29

9 This is considered in detail in **Chapter 3**

expressly refers to the transferor as being the person who ceases to carry out the relevant activities, rather than the employing entity (which is the approach adopted in the ARD).

However, it would be brave for a party involved in an SPC to rely on this technicality, to avoid TUPE applying. Although *Albron* is strictly only relevant to Regulation 3(1)(a) transfers, it is difficult to see how the logic behind it in safeguarding employee rights would not apply to SPCs as well. Otherwise, it would be simple to implement avoidance tactics to bypass the automatic transfer principle and associated employee protections.

In contrast, it is likely to be more difficult to argue that it applies an individual employed by an external third party, rather than a group entity. This may include, for example, those employed by an agency or providing services through their own personal service company or an umbrella arrangement. It is quite a different proposition to infer a "non-contractual" employment relationship with an individual outside the transferor's wider organisation and, it is submitted, would stretch the *Albron* principle beyond its limits. However, consideration should be given to whether the contractual employer could still be deemed a "sub-contractor" which may fall within an SPC[10].

Assigned to the organised grouping of resources or employees

TUPE will only apply to employees who are "assigned" to the transferring economic entity or, in the case of an SPC, the client team that has been deliberately put together for the principal purpose of performing the transferring services.

---

10 See **Chapter 5**

This is a long-standing principle established by ECJ case law[11] which is now enshrined in Regulation 4(1).

In practice, an assessment of how employees spend their time is used as the principal means for determining whether they are caught by a TUPE transfer. Many employers will treat anyone who spends more than 50%-60% of their working hours on the transferring activities as "assigned" and in scope to transfer (although this can be fluid, depending on the parties' respective commercial objectives).

This approach is usually intended to provide some commercial certainty, particularly when seeking to pin down a list of transferring employees to enable effective consultation to take place or establish the scope of any negotiated indemnities. However, it is not a fool-proof method, particularly where time spent is not meticulously recorded and an employee's work priorities may vary from week to week. Moreover, the legal test is more nuanced.

The decision in *Duncan Webb Offset (Maidstone) Ltd v. Cooper*[12] is a useful starting point, although the EAT was deliberately careful in its use of language. It declined to give definitive guidance due to the fact sensitivities of any particular case (an approach that has been replicated in subsequent judgments[13]). It went no further than saying it was *"quite prepared to accept"* that some or all of the following *"may well fall for consideration"*, as part of a non-exhaustive list:

> *"the amount of time spent on one part of the business or the other; the amount of value given to each part by the employee; the terms of the contract of employment showing what the employee could be required*

---

11 *Botzen and ors v. Rotterdamsche Droogdok Maatshappij BV* C-186/83, [1985] ECR 519 (ECJ)

12 [1995] IRLR 633 (EAT)

13 For example, see *Seawell Ltd v. Ceva Freight (UK) Ltd and anor* [2012] IRLR 802 (EAT), paragraph 47

> *to do; how the cost to the employer of the employee's services had been allocated between different parts of the business."*[14]

As noted above, there may be a dispute over who transfers and who stays behind and the question of "assignment" will frequently be key to this.

It would be very difficult to argue that an employee who is 90%+ dedicated to the transferring business or activities is not "assigned". But the more an employee splits their time between various transferring and non-transferring activities, the more the other factors will come into play.

In any event, it will often be almost impossible to determine what percentage of time is spent by an employee on any given task or work-type, which may vary (perhaps considerably) from week-to-week or month-to-month. So whilst it is envisaged that this will continue to be used as the primary benchmark in practice, the EAT's reasoning in *Duncan Webb* is sufficiently non-committal to offer considerable scope for creative argument.

Finally, Regulation 2(1) clarifies that "assigned" means *"assigned other than on a temporary basis"*. This will require a careful factual analysis in certain cases, where the distinction between a short-term arrangement and a discrete but longer-term project (or series of projects) may be blurred. The BIS Guide identifies the length of time the employee has been there and whether the transferor has identified a date for potential return or reassignment as potentially relevant factors[15].

---

14 *Duncan Webb*, at paragraph 15

15 BIS Guide, page 14

Assigned immediately before the transfer

Under Regulation 4(3), the issue of assignment needs to be assessed in relation to both: (a) employees assigned to the organised grouping of resources of employees immediately before the transfer; and (b) those who would have been, had they not been dismissed pre-transfer.

Although the parties to a commercial transaction will typically pre-agree a list of transferring employees, this will not be definitive or binding. There is always a residual risk of employees who are not on the list transferring (or, at least, alleging that they transfer). They are sometimes described as "wrong pocket" or "woodwork" employees and any liabilities associated with their inadvertent transfer are often covered by indemnities.

Due consideration should also be given to employees who are on long-term absence at the point of transfer (as this does not preclude them from being "assigned"). In *Fairhurst Ward Abbotts Ltd v. Botes Building Ltd and ors*[16], the Court of Appeal confirmed that an employee absent on sick leave remains a person employed in the relevant undertaking, even though they are not actually at work. The same applies to those on sabbatical, maternity leave and other forms of family-related leave (for example). In *BT Managed Services Ltd v. Edwards and anor*[17], the EAT subsequently sought to distinguish "permanent inability" (which it said would bring someone outside TUPE) from "temporary inability" (which would not). However, this should be treated with extreme caution.

Eagle-eyed readers will have noted that Regulation 4(1) refers specifically to employees whose contracts "*would otherwise be terminated by the transfer*". This is a curious piece of drafting that does not reflect any wording in the ARD and does not seem to add much of value. The transfer takes effect automatically by operation of law, unless the employee objects. It does not occur as an alternative to termination of

16 [2004] IRLR 304 (CA)

17 [2015] IRLR 994 (EAT)

employment. If there is no transfer, the transferor may need to decide whether to retain the employee on other work or consider termination, but Regulation 4(1) is not engaged either way.

There is also nothing in the legislation to prevent a transferor from redeploying employees who might otherwise transfer to another part of the business or a different customer account before the transfer takes place, to bring them outside the scope of TUPE[18].

Similarly, there is no legal prohibition on a transferor assigning employees to a particular client team or business function shortly before the transfer, so that they transfer out. For this reason, we will often see express provisions in a services contract which restrict the service provider's freedom to move employees onto or off the services for a period prior to termination, unless the customer consents[19].

Former employees of the transferor will be caught if they would have been assigned immediately before the transfer, but for their automatic unfair dismissal under Regulation 7(1), where the principal reason for termination is the transfer. This preserves TUPE protection for those who are dismissed before the transfer takes place, to avoid them otherwise transferring. They will be entitled to claim unfair dismissal (provided, of course, they have at least two years' continuous service) and such liability will transfer to the transferee.

In this regard, Regulation 4(3) codifies the previous position at common law, established by the House of Lords in *Litster v. Forth Dry Dock & Engineering Co Ltd*[20].

---

18 This is reflected in the BIS Guide, page 15

19 See **Chapter 18**

20 [1989] IRLR 161 (HL)

CHAPTER SEVEN

AUTOMATIC TRANSFER OF RIGHTS AND LIABILITIES

If an employee falls within the scope of TUPE, most pre-transfer liabilities, rights and duties are automatically dragged along with them and become the responsibility of the transferee.

In effect, the transferee steps into the shoes of the transferor and the employee's employment carries on as before.

This default position is often modified in practice, by warranty or indemnity provisions that may be negotiated between buyer and seller (in the case of a business or asset transaction) or between customer and service provider (in relation to a service provision change).

Although the parties cannot contract out of TUPE and the automatic transfer principle, they can seek to manage its impact and apportion liability between themselves as a matter of contract. The detail of the commercial arrangements will ultimately reflect their respective business objectives and bargaining power. This is considered in more detail in **Chapters 18 to 21**.

Key principles

Regulation 4(2) states that, subject to certain exceptions:

> *"on the completion of a relevant transfer:*
>
> *(a) all of the transferor's rights, powers, duties and liabilities under or in connection with any such contract shall be transferred by virtue of this regulation to the transferee; and*

> *(b) any act or omission before the transfer is completed, of or in relation to the transferor in respect of that contract or a person assigned to that organised grouping of resources or employees, shall be deemed to have been an act or omission of or in relation to the transferee."*

Unless agreed otherwise (and subject to certain limited exceptions), the transferee will take on liability for anything done or not done in respect of the transferring employees, whether before or after the transfer. This encompasses statutory, contractual and tortious claims that an employee may have against the transferor.

Automatic transfer principle

This automatic transfer principle is, at its heart, relatively straightforward.

The concept of "transfer" means what it says – the transferor can wash its hands of any liability, which will rest with the transferee (even though no fault can be attributed specifically to the transferee). This was confirmed by the EAT in *Ibex Trading Co. Ltd (in administration) v. Walton and ors*[1]:

> *"the use of the word 'transfer' in its natural and ordinary meaning suggests a taking away from one and a handing over to another. This is more consistent with the transferee taking on obligations in place of the transferor than that the transferor retains liability."*[2]

It will include, for example:

- liability for any pre-transfer decision by the transferor to terminate employment (and the underlying reasons for it) or not pay certain sums to the employee, or any behaviour by the

1 [1994] IRLR 564 (EAT)

2 *Ibex*, paragraph 6

transferor or its employees that might give rise to discrimination or other claims[3];

- some discretionary rights provided to employees by the transferor, which may not be contractual but still arise *"in connection with"* the contract of employment[4]. In these instances, it seems likely that the obligation on the employer will be to exercise its discretion rationally[5], taking into account relevant factors and disregarding irrelevant factors[6];

- liability for personal injury sustained by an employee pre-transfer[7], or where a post-transfer personal injury was caused by a breach occurring pre-transfer[8]. The transferee will be able to rely on the transferor's employer's liability insurance which, subject to some exceptions, is compulsory for every employer carrying out business in Great Britain[9];

- continuity of employment (for determining eligibility for unfair dismissal protection and statutory redundancy pay)[10] and length of service (which will be relevant, for example, in calculating statutory notice periods and statutory redundancy pay)[11].

---

3 See, for example, *DJM International Ltd v. Nicholas* [1996] IRLR 76 (EAT)

4 *The Proctor & Gamble Company and ors v. Svenska Cellulosa Aktiebolaget SCA and anor* [2012] IRLR 733 (Ch)

5 *Commerzbank AG v. Keen* [2007] ICR 623 (CA)

6 *Braganza v. BP Shipping Ltd* [2015] ICR 449 (UKSC)

7 *Bernadone v. Pall Mall Services Group and ors* [2000] IRLR 487 (CA)

8 *Baker v. British Gas Services (Commercial) Ltd and anor* [2017] EWHC 2302 (QBD)

9 s.1(1) Employers Liability (Compulsory Insurance) Act 1969

10 This is dealt with outside TUPE, in s.218(2) ERA 1996

11 *Collino and Chiappero v. Telecom Italia SpA* C-343/98,[2000] IRLR 788 (ECJ)

Similarly, the employees will owe their express and implied contractual employment obligations to the transferee, not the transferor.

Exceptions and qualifications

There are various instances in which the automatic transfer principle does not apply at all, or only applies to a limited extent:

- under Regulation 4(6), criminal liability does not transfer to the transferee;
- under Regulation 4A, where a collective agreement applies to a transferring employee, any provision agreed after the transfer date will not transfer if the transferee is not a participant in the collective bargaining for that provision. The treatment of trade union recognition and collective agreements is considered in **Chapter 11**;
- under Regulation 10, certain rights under an occupational pension scheme do not transfer. This includes benefits for old age, invalidity and survivors[12] and the right to bring claims for breach of contract or constructive unfair dismissal relating to a loss of rights under any such scheme[13]. The treatment of pensions in the context of TUPE transfers is complex and considered separately in **Chapter 12**;
- under Regulation 8(7), it does not apply where the transferor is subject to terminal insolvency proceedings, such as bankruptcy or liquidation. However, TUPE may still be relevant to non-terminal insolvencies (such as the sale of a business out of administration). This is considered in more detail in **Chapter 13**;

---

12 Regulation 10(2)

13 Regulation 10(3)

- entitlements to bonuses, benefits and share incentives will transfer, but there may be challenges in practice for the transferee in replicating certain types of incentive scheme. This is considered in **Chapter 14**;

- Similarly, the employer's right to enforce restrictive covenants will be inherited by the transferee, but it may be of limited value in practice. This is considered in **Chapter 15**;

- under Regulation 15(9), the transferor and transferee are jointly and severally liable for failures to inform or consult with employee representatives. This is considered in more detail in **Chapter 17**; and

- similarly, under Regulation 17(2), where the transferor is not required to put in place compulsory employer's liability insurance (for example, in the public sector), the transferor and transferee are jointly and several liable for any personal injury claim.

CHAPTER EIGHT

TERMINATING EMPLOYMENT

As the name suggests, one of the fundamental purposes of TUPE is the "protection of employment". There are substantial safeguards in place for employees whose employment is terminated in the context of TUPE. These may apply to pre- and post-transfer dismissals and regardless of whether it is the transferor, transferee or the employee who triggers termination.

TUPE does not, of itself, invalidate a dismissal or compel the transferee to continue employing an individual who transfers (or would otherwise have transferred). The "protection" given to employees comprises the existing remedies available for unfair dismissal (basic and compensatory awards or, in rare cases, reinstatement or re-engagement) and wrongful dismissal (contractual damages).

Four categories of termination

There are four separate categories of termination to consider:

1. Automatic unfair dismissal: The dismissal of an employee will be treated as automatically unfair if the sole or principal reason for the dismissal is the transfer itself, unless it is for an economic, technical or organisational reason entailing changes in the workforce (known commonly as an "ETO reason").

2. Employee's right to object: An individual has the right to object to the transfer voluntarily. Unless they have grounds for a claim under Regulation 4(9) or 4(11) below, their contract is

terminated but they are not treated as "dismissed" (meaning that they have no unfair dismissal protection).

3. Regulation 4(9) dismissal: An employee has the right to resign and claim unfair dismissal where the transfer involves (or would involve) a substantial change to their working conditions to their material detriment.

4. Constructive dismissal: An employee retains the right to resign without notice and claim they have been constructively (and unfairly) dismissed, in response to a repudiatory breach of contract.

For categories 1, 3 and 4 above, unfair dismissal protection will only apply to individuals who: (a) are classified as "employees" under the ERA 1996; and (b) have at least two years' continuous service[1]. There is no protection for those who are "workers" under the ERA 1996, even if they fall within the TUPE definition of "employee"[2].

Automatic unfair dismissal

When considering the issue of unfair dismissal in the context of a TUPE transfer, a three-step process can be adopted:

1. Is the transfer itself the sole or principal reason for dismissal?

2. If yes, is there a valid ETO reason?

3. If yes, is the dismissal nevertheless unfair, applying ordinary principles of unfair dismissal?

---

1 This is confirmed by Regulation 7(6). There are also a few other (very limited) exceptions where automatic unfair dismissal will not apply, in Regulations 7(5) and 7(6).

2 See **Chapter 6** for a discussion on the definition of "employee" for TUPE purposes, under Regulation 2(1).

(1) *Transfer as sole or principal reason for dismissal*

Regulation 7(1) states that:

> *"Where either before or after a relevant transfer, any employee of the transferor or transferee is dismissed, that employee is to be treated for the purposes of Part 10 of the [ERA 1996] (unfair dismissal) as unfairly dismissed if the sole or principal reason for the dismissal is the transfer."*

This principle (and the ETO reason exception considered below) is derived directly from Article 4(1) of the ARD.

Previously, the scope of automatic unfair dismissal was formulated more widely, to include cases where dismissal was for a reason "connected with the transfer". This was removed in 2014, meaning that the test is narrower than before.

As with many aspects of TUPE, whether the transfer itself is the *"sole or principal reason"* for dismissal requires a careful factual analysis. Once an employee has produced some evidence to support a case for automatic unfair dismissal, the burden rests with the employer to prove otherwise[3].

The Court of Appeal has confirmed that the close proximity of the dismissal to the transfer is not conclusive, but it is often strong evidence that the decision was taken because of the transfer[4].

In fact, a dismissal can still fall within Regulation 7(1), even if it occurs a considerable time before or after the transfer, provided that a causal link can be established between the two. In *London Metropolitan University v. Sackur and ors*[5], dismissals occurring two years after a TUPE transfer were deemed to be automatically unfair, following

---

3 *Marshall v. Game Retail Ltd* UKEAT/0276/12 (EAT)

4 *Hare Wines Ltd v. Kaur and anor* [2019] IRLR 555 (CA)

5 UKEAT/0286/06 (EAT)

attempts by the employer to move employees who had transferred to it in onto new employment contracts.

More generally, it will be important to look very carefully at the precise motivation for dismissal. For example, employment may be terminated in anticipation of a future TUPE transfer, but before a specific transferee has been identified. This scenario has been considered in the context of insolvency[6], where immediate steps may need to be taken to reduce costs and improve the viability of a struggling business for onward sale.

In *Spaceright Europe Ltd v. Baillavoine*[7], the CEO of Spaceright was dismissed on the day that administrators were appointed. At that time, the administrators had no specific sale transaction on the table and no prospective buyers to talk to. Regardless of this, the Court of Appeal determined that his dismissal was for a reason "connected with" the transfer (albeit not the transfer itself), when the business was sold a month later.

Spaceright pre-dates the 2014 amendments to TUPE, so it is debatable whether the same decision would be reached now, based on the current (narrower) formulation of Regulation 7(1). Indeed, in *Kavanagh and ors v. Crystal Palace FC and anor*[8], the Court of Appeal noted (on different, but analogous facts relating to insolvency) that it was:

> *"common ground that the principal reason for the dismissals was not 'the transfer itself' because, at the effective date of termination, no agreement had been reached in relation to the transfer".*

However, I am not convinced this will always be the case. Where an employee is dismissed to assist in convincing a prospective buyer to purchase the assets of a business (which may well constitute a TUPE

6 The interaction between TUPE and different types of insolvency is considered in **Chapter 13**

7 [2012] IRLR 111 (CA)

8 [2014] IRLR 139 (CA)

transfer), it is perfectly arguable that the sole or principal reason for such dismissal might be the transfer itself. It will depend on the facts and, as we will see later, in such circumstances an ETO reason is unlikely to apply. Therefore, *Spaceright* still warrants some caution.

Regulation 7(1) applies to *"any employee"* of the transferor or transferee, which includes who are not within the scope of a TUPE transfer. It would cover, for example, those left behind at the transferor post-transfer or those already employed by the transferee. I am not aware of any cases where an employee has been automatically unfairly dismissed because of a transfer that did not involve them. The most probable cause for dismissal in such circumstances would be redundancy, where there is likely to be an ETO reason.

(2) ETO reason

Under Regulation 7(2), there is no automatic unfair dismissal:

> *"where the sole or principal reason for the dismissal is an economic, technical or organisational reason entailing changes in the workforce of either the transferor or the transferee before or after a relevant transfer"*

There is surprisingly little judicial guidance (either at domestic or European level) regarding what constitutes an "economic, technical or organisational reason". The BIS Guide[9] suggests that:

- "economic" means *"a reason relating to the profitability or market performance of the new employer's business"*. However, it must relate to a continuation of the conduct of the business, rather than for the purpose of selling it[10];

- "technical" means *"a reason relating to the nature of the equipment or production processes which the new employer*

[9] BIS Guide, page 23

[10] *Spaceright*, paragraph 47

operates". This might include, for example, a decision to introduce new technologies which, in turn, reduces the need for human labour; and

- "organisational" means *"a reason relating to the management or organisational structure of the new employer's business"*. This might apply, for example, to a restructuring process resulting from post-transfer integration of transferring employees into the transferee's existing workforce.

There must also be a "change in the workforce" (otherwise, the ETO reason exception does not apply). This question needs to be considered in the context of the body of transferring employees as a whole, but not necessarily the transferee's entire wider workforce[11]. It could be a change in:

- the numbers employed in the workforce[12] – in other words, a classic redundancy situation where the transferee's requirements for work of a particular kind have ceased or diminished;

- job functions[13] – for example, where the same number of employees are required but different roles or skills are needed post-transfer. A minor change to the functions of a small group of employees may not be sufficient[14]; and

- location[15] – this will cover a place of work redundancy, where the transferee intends to carry out the relevant activities in a different location to the transferor. This may be particularly relevant where outsourced services are moved overseas, or where

---

11 *Nationwide Building Society v. Benn and ors* [2010] IRLR 922 (EAT)

12 *Berriman v. Delabole Slate Ltd* [1985] IRLR 305 (CA)

13 *Berriman (as above)*

14 *Green v. Elan Care Ltd* UKEAT/18/01 (EAT)

15 Regulation 7(3A)

a relocation of work does not fall within the bounds of a reasonable contractual mobility clause.

Generally, an ETO reason will not apply if a dismissal is made not with a view to the future conduct of the business, but simply to make the onward sale of a business more attractive to potential suitors. However, there is a fine line between this and terminating employment in order to reduce costs and enable the business to continue trading on a skeleton staff, in the hope of a future sale (which can be an ETO reason)[16].

Importantly, the transferor cannot rely on the transferee's ETO reason to effect dismissals, before the transfer takes place[17].

This may arise, for example, when activities are being transferred to a new location, resulting in a place of work redundancy (assuming that there is no appetite for a transferring employee to relocate). However, if the employees are dismissed by the outgoing employer pre-transfer (as might appear logical), this will be automatically unfair.

The correct approach, at least in terms of TUPE compliance, is for the transferee to deal with redundancies post-transfer (although, if relevant, there is scope for collective redundancy consultation to begin pre-transfer[18]). This can cause a practical headache, particularly if the work is moving overseas and the transferee has no UK presence. I explain how this issue can be navigated commercially, in the context of a cross-border transfer, in **Chapter 19**.

---

16 *Kavanagh*, paragraph 28 – distinguishing the facts in *Kavanagh* to those in *Spaceright*

17 *Hynd v. Armstrong* [2007] IRLR 338 (CSIH)

18 ss.198A and 198B TULR(C)A 1992 – discussed in **Chapter 17**

(3) Application of ordinary unfair dismissal principles

If there is a valid ETO reason, there is no automatic unfair dismissal. However, the ordinary principles of unfair dismissal will still apply.

The potentially fair reason for dismissal will be deemed to be either redundancy (under s.98(2)(c) ERA 1996) or "some other substantial reason" (under s.98(1)(b) ERA 1996) and the fairness of any such dismissal will be considered in accordance with s.98(4) ERA 1996[19].

If the dismissal occurs post-transfer, the transferee still needs to follow a fair process (including consulting individually with affected employees regarding a proposed redundancy and considering suitable alternative roles). This may require it to, amongst other things, pool employees it has inherited via TUPE with members of its existing workforce, where they perform similar roles.

If the dismissal occurs pre-transfer but is not automatically unfair, either because: (a) the sole or principal reason is not the transfer itself, under Regulation 7(1); or (b) the transferor has an ETO reason under Regulation 7(2), ordinary unfair dismissal principles will still apply but liability does not transfer to the transferee[20].

Employee's right to object

Although TUPE operates to transfer automatically the contract of employment of an affected employee, it does not compel the employee to work for the transferee. The right of an individual to choose their employer freely remains unaffected and they can simply decide not to transfer.

Regulation 4(7) states that TUPE:

19 Regulation 7(3)(b)

20 *Thompson v. SCS Consulting Ltd and ors* [2001] IRLR 801 (EAT)

> *"shall not operate to transfer the contract of employment and the rights, powers, duties and liabilities under or in connection with it of an employee who informs the transferor or the transferee that he objects to becoming employed by the transferee."*

As the statutory wording suggests, the employee must give a clear indication that they do not wish to move to the new employer. They must genuinely object to being transferred[21]. There is no requirement for an objection to be communicated in writing (although typically, it will be) and there are no other specific formalities.

An employee can object after the transfer, if they do not know the identity of the transferee pre-transfer[22].

Regulation 4(8) states that:

> *"Subject to paragraphs (9) and (11), where an employee so objects, the relevant transfer shall operate so as to terminate his contract of employment with the transferor but he shall not be treated, for any purpose, as having been dismissed by the transferor."*

Although it is possible for the employee to remain with the transferor after they have objected, the effect of Regulation 4(8) means that they would need to be re-engaged separately under a new contract. The BIS Guide suggests that this would break continuity of employment[23]. However, this appears to be inconsistent with the statutory principles relating to continuous employment in ERA 1996[24], which require there to be *"a week which does not count"* to break continuity[25]. Assuming re-engagement occurs sufficiently quickly, there seems no reason why an employee could not rely on continuous service.

---

21 See, for example, *Capita Health Solutions v. McLean* [2008] IRLR 595 (EAT)

22 *New ISG Ltd v. Vernon* [2008] IRLR 45 (Ch)

23 BIS Guide, page 13

24 Part XIV, Chapter I ERA 1996 (ss.210-219)

25 s.210(4) ERA 1996

A similar result can be achieved by the transferor redeploying the employee elsewhere within its business, so that they are not assigned to the organised grouping of resources or employees immediately before the transfer. In practice, this will be subject to any contractual limitation on the transferor's ability to move employees around (or, indeed, a contractual obligation on the transferor to redeploy, to give effect to the parties' intention that TUPE should not apply).

As a starting point, an objecting employee has no right to claim unfair dismissal, notice pay or any other form of compensation arising from the termination. This is subject to their right to resign and claim that they have been dismissed under Regulation 4(9) or Regulation 4(11), which are considered below.

Regulation 4(9) dismissal

Regulation 4(9) states that:

> *"where a relevant transfer involves or would involve a substantial change in working conditions to the material detriment of a person whose contract of employment is or would be transferred under paragraph (1), such an employee may treat the contract of employment as having been terminated, and the employee shall be treated for any purpose as having been dismissed by the employer."*

This provision transposes the requirements of Article 4(2) of the ARD. It is subject to the rules on insolvency proceedings in Regulation 9 where, in certain circumstances, the transferee can make changes to an employee's terms and conditions to safeguard employment opportunities and ensure the survival of the business. This is considered in more detail in **Chapter 13**.

Regulation 4(9) creates an additional right for an employee to resign and claim unfair dismissal protection, unique to the TUPE context. The bar is set lower than for orthodox constructive unfair dismissal claims, which require the employer to have committed a repudiatory breach of contract. This is covered separately in Regulation 4(11).

Under Regulation 4(9), there may, in fact, be no breach of contract at all. A transferee might choose, for example, to discontinue certain discretionary benefits to which the employee has no express or implied contractual right. The only requirements are that the change in working conditions must be *"substantial"* and cause the employee to suffer a *"material detriment"*.

In practice, this issue may arise where the transferee seeks to rely on a contractual mobility clause to invoke a change in work location. There are a number of cases which help to illustrate how Regulation 4(9) principles are applied in this specific context.

In *Tapere v South London and Maudsley NHS Trust*[26], a change in workplace resulted in an increased journey time for the claimant, which had a knock-on effect on her childcare arrangements (even though the distance between old and new locations was only 2.5 miles). The EAT was clear that the *"material detriment"* test was not an objective one and *"what has to be considered is the impact of the proposed change from the employee's point of view"*[27].

Similarly, in *Abellio London Ltd v. Musse and ors*[28], London bus drivers were relocated from a Westbourne Park bus depot to one in Battersea. This involved additional travel of between one and two hours per day for each affected employee. This fell squarely within the remit of Regulation 4(9).

However, this can be compared to *Cetinsoy and ors v. London United Busways*[29], where bus drivers were moved from Westbourne Park to another depot at Stamford Brook. This resulted in additional travel

26 [2009] IRLR 972 (EAT)

27 *Tapere*, paragraph 53

28 [2012] IRLR 360 (EAT)

29 UKEAT/0042/14 (EAT)

time of 30 to 60 minutes per day. Interestingly, this will not held to be a *"substantial change"* to working conditions, because Stamford Brook was still more convenient than any of the five other locations which they could have been required to move (even before the transfer), under the specific express terms of their contract.

Under Regulation 4(10), no damages are payable in relation to a Regulation 4(9) dismissal *"in respect of any failure by the employer to pay wages to an employee in respect of a notice period which the employee has failed to work"*.

This is a curious anomaly, which does not apply to other types of TUPE-related dismissal. A well-advised employee seeking to rely on Regulation 4(9) will resign on notice, rather than walk out immediately. This will enable them to preserve their notice pay but still retain the right to claim unfair dismissal compensation for financial losses arising after the notice period.

Any liability for Regulation 4(9) claims will transfer to the transferee, as it only applies to employees whose contract of employment transfers or would transfer to the transferee. It is difficult to envisage a situation where any such dismissal is not by reason of the transfer itself and, even if there is an ETO reason, it will not be the transferor's reason.

Constructive dismissal

Regulation 4(11) states that the automatic transfer principle (Regulation 4(1)), an employee's right to object (Regulation 4(7)) and an employee's right to treat themselves as having been dismissed under Regulation 4(9) are:

> *"without prejudice to any right of an employee arising apart from these Regulations to terminate his contract of employment without notice in acceptance of a repudiatory breach of contract by his employer."*

Unlike Regulation 4(9), it is not confined to transferring employees. In theory, it can also be invoked by employees who are not in-scope and remain with the transferor post-transfer. In practice, this does not add anything and simply reflects the status quo, as such employees would only have a claim against the transferor in any event.

Similarly, if an employee has already transferred under TUPE, their "employer" is the transferee who would remain responsible for any repudiatory breach of contract.

However, the question of who is liable for pre-transfer constructive dismissal claims brought by employees who would otherwise have transferred is a little more complex.

In *University of Oxford v. Humphreys*[30], the Court of Appeal held that where an employee objects to the transfer in response to the transferee's proposed repudiatory breach of contract, any liabilities in connection with their contract do not transfer but they preserve the right to bring a constructive dismissal claim against the transferor.

This is undoubtedly correct (given the wording of Regulation 4(8)), but it seems counter-intuitive. The transferee may be at fault for creating the circumstances that result in the repudiatory breach of contract, but the transferor is deemed responsible. It is a mirror image of the normal position under TUPE where, under Regulation 4(2)(b), the transferee assumes liability for anything which is the transferor's fault.

It appears that the principle in *Humphreys* only applies if the employee invokes the right to object to the transfer under Regulation 4(7), in conjunction with their constructive dismissal claim. If the employee resigns pre-transfer but does not also clearly communicate that they object to the transfer, liability passes to the transferee in the normal way. Similarly, the transferee is likely to be liable for a constructive dismissal arising from a pre-transfer repudiatory breach by the transferor.

---

30 [2000] IRLR 183 (CA)

Constructive dismissal is entirely separate to any rights an employee may have under Regulation 4(9). Therefore, a prudent claimant may choose to bring both claims in the alternative. If they are unable to establish a repudiatory breach under Regulation 4(11), they still have the chance to satisfy the lower threshold of Regulation 4(9). If they have formally objected to the transfer as well, they can name both transferor and transferee as co-respondents (in case *Humphreys* applies).

CHAPTER NINE

CHANGING TERMS OF EMPLOYMENT

The restriction on varying terms and conditions in the context of a TUPE transfer is a significant statutory interference with the parties' ability to contract freely.

Alongside protection from dismissal, it is the cornerstone of the principle that employees' rights should be safeguarded. However, in one sense it is more radical.

TUPE does not render a dismissal void. It provides access to a remedy for those who are unfairly dismissed (which will usually involve financial compensation, rather than re-instatement or re-engagement). However, it does not compel an employer to keep an employee in a role it does not want or need.

Conversely, if a purported change to an employment contract contravenes TUPE, it simply has no effect (even if the employee agrees to it). This has wide-ranging commercial implications.

The transferee must accept the transferring employees as they are, even if their rights and benefits differ materially from those offered to its existing workforce. They may have to operate a multi-tiered workforce, with employees performing ostensibly the same work on different remuneration structures. There is the obvious potential for those on less favourable terms to be disgruntled or disengaged, causing tensions within the workforce. This can be a headache for employers who are involved regularly in TUPE transfers, as contracts are won and lost.

An incoming service provider will need to price according to the employee costs it inherits, where the ability to run a lean, affordable service may be the motivation for the customer outsourcing or re-tendering the work. As we will see, the spectre of future contractual variations falling foul of TUPE will linger for a considerable time after the transfer.

Therefore, these rules may significantly hamper a new bidder's ability to deliver any required cost savings at an acceptable margin, unless they can be creative in finding operational savings elsewhere. It may force them to change how the services are performed (potentially bringing any transfer outside the SPC rules) or, contrary to TUPE's purpose of protecting employment, make transferring employees redundant because they are too expensive. .

Key principles

The ARD does not state explicitly that TUPE-related contractual variations are void. However, Article 3(1), which confirms that the transferor's rights and obligations arising from a contract of employment or employment relationship are transferred to the transferee, has been interpreted in this way by the ECJ[1].

This principle is reflected in Regulation 4(4):

> *"Subject to Regulation 9, any purported variation of a contract of employment that is, or will be, transferred by [Regulation 4(1)], is void if the sole or principal reason for the variation is the transfer."*

As a reminder, Regulation 4(1) deals with the automatic transfer of employees, where their contracts are stated to have effect as if originally made with the transferee. This is considered in **Chapter 6**.

1 *Rask and anor v. ISS Kantineservice A/S* C-209/21, [1993] IRLR 133 (ECJ), applying the principles in *Foreningen af Arbejdslere i Danmark v. Daddy's Dance Hall A/S* C-324/86, [1988] IRLR 315 (ECJ)

Regulation 9 deals with certain permitted variations of contract in the context of non-terminal insolvency proceedings (such as an administration). This is considered in **Chapter 13**.

There are three main exceptions. Changes to terms and conditions of employment introduced because of a TUPE transfer are not automatically void if:

- there is an economic, technical or organisational reason entailing changes in the workforce (or "ETO reason"). This is the same ETO reason exception that applies to dismissals, although it has more limited scope in the context of varying terms of employment;
- they are made in accordance with an existing contractual right to vary terms; or
- the variation relates to a collectively agreed term and takes effect more than a year after the transfer, provided that the employee's terms are no less favourable overall.

Transfer as sole or principal reason

Similar to the rules on dismissals, the scope of protection against TUPE-related changes to contractual terms was previously formulated more widely, to include cases where they were made for a reason "connected with the transfer". This was removed in 2014.

What is the real reason?

There will need to be careful consideration of the underlying motivation for changing terms, to identify whether there is sufficient causal link such that the transfer itself is the *"sole or principal reason"*.

This issue will typically arise where there is a strategic decision by the transferee to harmonise employment terms post-transfer, to bring transferring employees in line with the rest of its workforce. Introducing changes for the purpose of harmonisation does not circumvent the restrictions imposed by TUPE and the ARD, if the underlying reason is the transfer[2].

Therefore, where a transferee wishes to implement changes for transferring employees, it is usually well-advised to wait until there another business reason which is independent of the TUPE transfer itself. This opportunity might arise as part of a future pay review exercise or, in certain individual cases, a promotion.

However, it is not always as straightforward as waiting for the next annual pay review (or indeed, the one after that). The mere passage of time may not, of itself, be sufficient. As we have already seen in one case, a gap of two years did not break the causal link[3].

The BIS Guide confirms that it requires an assessment of all the factual circumstances:

> *"There is no 'rule of thumb' used by the courts or specified in the Regulations to define a period of time after which it is safe to assume that the transfer did not impact directly or indirectly on the employer's actions."*[4]

This leaves a transferee in a difficult no-man's land. To adopt the BIS Guide's language, it is tricky to identify precisely when it is *"safe to assume"* that implementing contractual changes will be effective.

The EAT has confirmed that it is not correct to approach the issue by considering whether the changes would have been implemented "but for" for the transfer[5]. It is more nuanced than that. There may, in fact,

---

2 *Martin and ors v. South Bank University* C-4/01, [2004] IRLR 74 (ECJ)

3 *London Metropolitan University v. Sackur and ors* UKEAT/0286/06 (EAT) – discussed in **Chapter 8**

4 BIS Guide, page 24

5 *Smith and ors v. Trustees of Brooklands College* UKEAT/028/11 (EAT)

be a multitude of legitimate reasons, so the transfer is not the *"sole reason"*. However, the overarching context of TUPE can make it difficult in practice to create sufficient separation to ensure that it is not the *"principal reason"*.

The jeopardy remains that, even if a transferring employee accepts the new terms, this does not prevent them from reneging on that agreement in the future by claiming that the changes are automatically void[6].

The issue of cherry-picking

There is no principle in law that less favourable changes are permitted if they are cancelled out by more favourable terms introduced elsewhere by the transferee[7].

There has also been an important recent shift in the law, relating to changes that potentially operate to the benefit of the employee.

It used to be well-established that where a transferee purported to introduce contractual changes related to the transfer, the employee could "cherry pick". In effect, they could have the best of both worlds, by rejecting any less favourable terms offered by the transferee (and relying on their existing contract of employment) but still take advantage of the transferee's more generous terms where it suited them to do so.

This approach was based on the Court of Appeal's decision in *Regent Security Services Ltd v. Power*[8]. In *Power*, it was held that a transferee was not entitled to introduce a contractual change (in this case, increasing retirement age from 60 to 65) and then subsequently rely on TUPE to disapply it. However, *Power* was decided in relation to TUPE

6 *British Fuels Ltd v. Baxendale and anor; Wilson and ors v. St Helen's Borough Council* [1998] IRLR 706 (HL)

7 *Daddy's Dance Hall*, paragraph 15

8 [2008] IRLR 66 (CA)

1981, when the UK's approach to TUPE-related contractual changes was based solely on the interpretation of European case law. This has since been superseded by Regulation 4(4).

More recently, a different approach has been taken in *Ferguson and ors v. Astrea Asset Management Limited*[9]. This case involved a decision by directors of the transferor to award themselves substantially better financial terms before the transfer, which were then inherited by the transferee.

The EAT ruled that a proper interpretation of Regulation 4(4) rendered void <u>any</u> purported variation where the sole or principal reason is the transfer. It did not apply only to changes that were adverse to the employees.

This is directly contradictory to the BIS Guide, which states that *"Changes to terms and conditions agreed by the parties which are entirely positive are not prevented by the Regulations"*[10]. This is now clearly outdated and wrong.

In reaching its decision in *Astrea*, the EAT remarked that although allowing an employee to choose between two conflicting contractual terms may have worked for the employee in *Power*:

> *"this would not always be satisfactory and it would leave open the prospect that contractual rights would be dependent on the subjective view of the individual employee, who might change his mind at any time."*

The facts in *Astrea* were unusual, as the changes were implemented by the transferring employees themselves for their own benefit (and to the intended detriment of the transferee). Not only were they deemed void under Regulation 4(4), they also contravened the general EU abuse of law principle.

---

9 [2020] IRLR 577 (EAT)

10 BIS Guide, page 21

However, the EAT's decision reflects a trend in case law that TUPE and the ARD are not aimed solely at protecting employee rights. Rather, the purpose of the legislation is to ensure a fair balance between the interests of the transferring employees and the transferee[11]. This is more difficult to achieve, if the transferee is beholden to the changing whims of an employee regarding which terms they wish to apply.

It may be said that this leaves transferees in a potentially unenviable position, where they cannot guarantee that any changes they introduce will be effective, even if they are intended to improve the employee's position. However, in practice, it will likely work in their favour.

It seems unlikely that a transferring employee would challenge an obviously more favourable term (such as an enhanced benefits package). Conversely, it appears to leave open the possibility of a transferee rowing back on a TUPE-related variation that it no longer wishes to rely on, something that was previously not permitted under *Power*. This seems unfair to a transferring employee wishing to take advantage of a beneficial change post-transfer that the transferee put in place voluntarily, but it is consistent with *Astrea* and Regulation 4(4).

There may still be difficulties where there is a difference in views on whether a contractual variation is, in fact, beneficial. However, the only relevant test is whether the sole or principal reason for the variation was the transfer. If the employee wishes to argue that it is void, they will still need to demonstrate that it has been introduced because of the transfer and seek to rely on their old terms. In that sense, the right to cherry pick has not been entirely laid to rest by *Astrea*.

11 See *Alemo-Herron and ors v Parkwood Leisure Ltd* C-426/11, [2014] IRLR 744 (CJEU), paragraph 25. This principle was applied in the recent decision on fragmentation in *ISS Facility Services NV v. Govaerts and anor* C-344/18, [2020] IRLR 639 (CJEU) (discussed in **Chapter 10**).

A practical approach to risk

An effective way to mitigate the risks outlined above is for the transferee to prepare a clear, written commercial rationale for any changes that distances them from the transfer. Many responsible employers will already perform a similar exercise when seeking to demonstrate a business case for redundancy, or where it considers any proposed changes may be controversial (in case it has to resort to potential dismissal and re-engagement).

This should highlight the specific (non-transfer related) event which has given rise to the change and also explain the wider financial or organisational importance of implementing it. Reference could be made to any relevant economic, technical or organisational factors (even though the scope for arguing a valid ETO reason is limited). For example, changing or introducing restrictive covenants in the context of a promotion could be justified by the requirement for additional business protection, given the employee's increased seniority (and the threat posed if they were to leave).

It is not a guaranteed solution. However, if the employer has addressed its mind to these issues (and is seen to have done so), there is a better chance of demonstrating that the transfer was not the sole or principal reason.

A possible alternative, sometimes mooted in practice, is to dismiss the employees under a settlement agreement and then offer re-engagement on new terms, post-transfer. The theory is that any claims (including TUPE-related automatic unfair dismissal) are waived by the settlement agreement and the new terms cannot amount to a TUPE-related variation of contract, because the old contract no longer exists. This is certainly creative, but it carries legal risk.

The case that is often cited is *Solectron Scotland Ltd v. Roper and ors*[12]. This concerned a compromise (now settlement) agreement that settled

12 [2004] IRLR 4 (EAT)

claims arising from a post-transfer redundancy process, including contractual enhanced redundancy terms inherited from the transferor. The EAT concluded that the compromise agreement was not being used to implement a change to contractual redundancy pay, but simply to settle a dispute as to its value. Therefore, it did not amount to a transfer-related variation of contract, which would otherwise be void.

This decision has limited wider value, not least because in *Solectron*, the employees were made redundant and there was no subsequent offer to re-engage on new terms. *Solectron* does not establish a broader proposition that a settlement agreement followed by re-engagement is effective in bypassing Regulation 4(4).

Indeed, Regulation 18 is clear that the parties cannot agree to exclude or limit the operation of TUPE. This includes the use of settlement agreements to dismiss and re-engage.

The transferee could simply choose to dismiss and offer re-engagement without a settlement agreement. However, this is unlikely to be palatable in many cases, as it will inevitably lead to an automatically unfair dismissal for employees with at least two years' continuous service.

Permitted variations

A TUPE-related change to terms is still permitted in certain limited circumstances.

(1) ETO reason

Regulation 4(5)(a) states that Regulation 4(4) does not prevent a variation of the contract of contract if:

> *"the sole or principal reason for the variation is an economic, technical or organisational reason entailing changes in the workforce, provided that the employer and employee agree that variation."*

It is questionable whether this is compatible with the ARD, which only provides for the ETO reason defence in cases of dismissal[13]. However, in practice, an ETO reason is much less likely to apply to a change in contractual terms than it is to a TUPE-related dismissal.

Although the underlying reason may be economic, technical or organisational in nature, it must also satisfy the further requirement of *"entailing changes to the workforce"*. This means either a change in the numbers or job functions of employees[14], or a change in workplace[15]. It is difficult to envisage many circumstances where this would apply.

A change in numbers of employees typically involves a redundancy situation, and is therefore only likely to be applicable to a dismissal.

A variation caused by a change in job function will, in many cases, be covered by other provisions of TUPE. If the variation itself is a change in duties, it may already be permitted by an existing contractual term allowing the employer to assign alternative duties (and therefore fall within Regulation 4(5)(b)). If it relates to a variation as a consequence of a change in job function (such as a change in pay), it will still need to be agreed by the employee. And if the change in job function is, in itself, sufficiently significant, it may amount to a redundancy of the employee's existing role, with the new function being a potentially suitable alternative.

Similarly, a change in job location will either constitute a place of work redundancy or be permitted within the scope of an existing contractual mobility clause. A variation in pay caused by different local market rate applying in the new location may fall within the ETO reason defence, but again it still requires employee consent. In an international context,

---

13 Article 4(1)

14 *Berriman v. Delabole Slate Ltd* [1985] IRLR 305 (CA) – as discussed in **Chapter 8**

15 Regulation 4(5A)

it could be engaged where there is a transfer overseas and the employee is placed on a local contract[16].

(2) <u>Existing contractual right to vary</u>

Regulation 4(5)(b) states that Regulation 4(4) does not prevent a variation of the contract of contract if:

> *"the terms of that contract permit the employer to make such a variation."*

This exception does not sit easily with the European case law, which leaves no room for contractual changes where the reason is the transfer. For example, in *Daddy's Dance Hall*, the ECJ ruled that the purpose of the ARD:

> *"is to ensure that the rights resulting from a contract of employment or employment relationship of employees affected by the transfer of an undertaking are safeguarded. Since this protection is a matter of public policy... it is not possible to derogate from them in a manner unfavourable to employees."* [17]

The counter-argument is that any such variation is not because of the TUPE transfer, but because of an existing contractual right to vary which is simply preserved following the TUPE transfer. Regulation 4(5)(b) does no more than clarify that the transferee can continue to rely on it, in the same way as the transferor might previously have done.

Even if there is a unilateral power to vary terms, this will still be interpreted narrowly. In particular, a general flexibility clause is unlikely to allow the employer to make anything other than minor changes that are not to the employee's detriment.

---

16 See **Chapter 19**

17 *Daddy's Dance Hall*, paragraph 14

(3) Varying collectively agreed terms

In certain circumstances, a transferee will also be permitted to vary terms incorporated into the employment contract from a collective agreement. This is considered in **Chapter 11**.

Application of normal variation principles

If a proposed change is not automatically void, the normal principles relating to implementing contractual variations will still apply[18].

In summary, this means that the employer will require employee consent (unless it can rely on the limited scope of an existing contractual right to vary). If this is not forthcoming, the employer could attempt to force the changes through unilaterally (although this is rarely advisable) or, as a last resort, dismiss and offer re-engagement on the new terms. However, it will need to have a sound business reason and follow a fair process to mitigate the risk of unfair dismissal liability for employees with at least two years' service.

Additionally, the transferee will need to show that the purpose of dismissing and re-engaging was not simply to push through changes that would otherwise be void under Regulation 4(4). Otherwise, if the sole or principal reason for dismissal is deemed to be the transfer, it will be automatically unfair.

As we have seen, the transferee will not be able to rely on an ETO reason, unless it can show that it entails changes in the workforce. In *Hazel and anor v. The Manchester College*[19], the employees accepted re-engagement and worked under new terms which included a pay cut, but they were still able to claim automatic unfair dismissal. Subsequently, the Employment Tribunal awarded re-engagement on the new terms, save that their old pay was preserved.

---

[18] Regulation 4(5C)

[19] [2014] IRLR 392 (CA)

There may also be a requirement to engage in collective redundancy consultation with employee representatives, where there is a proposal to dismiss at least 20 employees in a 90-day period at one establishment[20].

Even if a change can otherwise be implemented lawfully, the employee still has the right to object to the transfer and/or resign and claim unfair dismissal under Regulation 4(9), on the basis that it amounts to a substantial change to their material detriment. This is considered in **Chapter 8**.

The impact of restricting variations to employment terms is considered separately in the context of pensions (**Chapter 12**), bonuses, benefits and share schemes (**Chapter 14**) and restrictive covenants (**Chapter 15**).

20 s.188 TULR(C)A 1992

PART C

TRICKY ISSUES

CHAPTER TEN

FRAGMENTATION

Sometimes, a transfer may involve more than one potential transferee. A business and its assets may be sold in separate lots to different buyers. A large outsourcing contract may be re-tendered and the services divided up between two or more new (and potentially competing) providers. In other words, the relevant economic entity or activities may become fragmented.

For many years, the law dealt with fragmentation in a sensible way. If the relevant test for the transfer of an economic entity or a service provision change was met, any TUPE transfer could only result in employees transferring to one of the putative transferees.

This was reasonably well-understood, if not always easy to advise on with certainty in practice. The question of assignment might be given sharper focus, with contrary views on whether certain employees should land in one destination or another. If an employee was not assigned to any specific organised grouping of resources or employees, they might fall through the gap and simply remain with the transferor.

However, this previous orthodoxy has been completely upended by two important recent judgments.

In *ISS Facility Services NV v. Govaerts and anor*[1], the CJEU ruled that, subject to certain conditions, employment contracts could be "split" on the transfer of an economic entity, leaving open the possibility that an employee's employment could transfer to multiple transferees.

---

1 C-344/18, [2020] IRLR 639 (CJEU)

In *McTear Contracts Ltd v. Bennett and ors*[2], the principles established in *Govaerts* were applied by the EAT to service provision changes.

The combined impact of these decisions has caused ripples of debate amongst employment lawyers. It has also left employers grappling with several challenging practical problems.

Govaerts: Transfer of an economic entity

In *Govaerts*, ISS was responsible for the cleaning and maintenance of various buildings in the picturesque Belgian city of Ghent, divided into Lot 1 (museums and historical buildings), Lot 2 (libraries and community centres) and Lot 3 (administrative buildings). Ms Govaerts was the project manager across all areas of work. Following a re-tendering process, Lots 1 and 3 (comprising approximately 85% of the work) were awarded to a new provider (Atalian) and Lot 2 was awarded to a different provider. A dispute arose when ISS maintained that Ms Govaerts' employment transferred to Atalian, but Atalian disagreed and refused to take her on.

The CJEU determined that "no transfer" was not the answer. Further, it was unreasonable to place all liability on Atalian, even if it took on the majority of the services. The purpose of the ARD was to ensure a fair balance between the interests of employees and the transferee[3].

Therefore, the CJEU concluded that:

> *"the rights and obligations arising from a contract of employment are* ***transferred to each of the transferees, in proportion to the tasks performed*** *by the worker concerned,* ***provided that the division of the contract of employment as a result of the transfer is possible and neither causes a worsening of working conditions nor***

2 [2021] IRLR 444 (EAT)

3 As established in *Alemo-Herron and ors v Parkwood Leisure Ltd* C-426/11, [2014] IRLR 744 (CJEU)

> ***adversely affects the safeguarding of the rights of workers...*** *If such a division were impossible to carry out or would adversely affect the rights of that worker, the transferee(s) would be regarded as being responsible for any consequent termination of the employment relationship... even if that termination were to be initiated by the worker."*[4] (emphasis added)

This is a significant new development. It provides that a single employment contract can, in principle, be split into two (or more) new employment contracts which take effect with different transferees, in proportion to the work performed on each transferring part. I will call this the "*Govaerts* principle".

Potentially, it results in a transferring employee having part-time employment contracts across multiple employers, with their existing terms and conditions preserved in each case. Prior to *Govaerts*, this approach had been dismissed by the EAT as *"truly novel"*[5] and roundly rejected by the Northern Ireland Court of Appeal as giving rise to *"insuperable difficulties"*[6].

Several legal and practical issues become immediately apparent, simply by considering the qualifications to the *Govaerts* principle identified by the CJEU itself.

Dividing the contract must be possible

This would appear to be a relatively low bar. Put another way, division would need to be impossible, to disapply the *Govaerts* principle at this initial hurdle.

Of course, it will be necessary to establish first that:

---

4 *Govaerts*, paragraph 38

5 *Kimberley Group Housing Ltd v. Hambley and ors* [2008] IRLR 682 (EAT)

6 *Hassard v. McGrath* [1996] NI 586 (NICA)

- there is a transfer of an economic entity, under Regulation 3(1)(a). This may not always be the case, where an entity is divided up and becomes so fragmented that it becomes difficult to identify whether certain parts have maintained their identity in the hands of the relevant transferees[7]; and

- the employee is assigned to the relevant organised grouping of resources – namely, the totality of the undertaking (or part) which is the subject of the transfer – before any split is considered. This requires consideration of a multitude of factors, as outlined in *Duncan Webb Offset (Maidstone) Ltd v. Cooper*[8].

If there is a transfer and the employee is assigned, the *Govaerts* principle operates to divide their contract, purely in proportion to the tasks performed. This may require nothing more than an analysis of how the employee spends their time. It is less nuanced than the assignment test in *Duncan Webb*, and the two should not be conflated.

In Ms Govaerts' circumstances, dividing her contract was relatively straightforward. There were only two transferees and her work was split relatively neatly – she spent two days per week on one part of the business and three days per week on the other. However, it will seldom be this clear-cut.

The proportion of tasks performed on various fragments of the transferring entity or services may vary from week to week, depending on short-term operational priorities or customer demand. Although a worker may be assigned to the relevant transferring economic entity, they may float between the various elements of it, whether by accident or design.

---

7 See *Fairhurst Ward Abbotts Ltd v. Botes Building Ltd and ors* [2004] IRLR 304 (CA), paragraph 41 – this is discussed in **Chapter 2**

8 [1995] IRLR 184 (EAT) – the issue of assignment is considered in detail in **Chapter 6**

Having more than two transferees may also complicate things. For example, how do you sensibly divide an employee's five-day working week between three transferees? And even assuming that can be done in theory, how do you get three potentially competing transferees (each with their own commercial priorities) to agree on the appropriate division? There may be a need to repeat that exercise for several transferring employees, with each individual having different levels of experience, skills, value to the business and employment costs. You can see the commercial negotiations getting bogged down quite quickly.

However, until we receive further judicial guidance, it is difficult to say with confidence that this type of practical challenge would be enough to disapply the *Govaerts* principle.

The issue of whether something is possible is very different to whether it is practicable. Presumably, *"possible"* should be given its ordinary natural meaning. In one sense, if the degree of fragmentation does not preclude a transfer in the first place, it may be difficult to demonstrate that it is impossible to work out how the contracts of any transferring employees should be divided amongst the various transferees.

Dividing the contract must not worsen working conditions or adversely affect the safeguarding of workers' rights

From the transferor's perspective, this may not matter. If a division of contracts does not adversely affect the employee, their employment transfers to multiple transferees. If it does, the transferees are responsible for any termination costs (unless there is a commercial agreement to apportion liability in another way).

It may also be possible for the employee to stay with the transferor, if that is desired. *Govaerts* does not state that termination would inevitably follow in all cases, merely that the transferee(s) *"would be regarded as being responsible for any consequent termination"*. But would an employee still be required to object to the transfer under Regulation 4(7), or would the transferor have to redeploy them pre-transfer?

For transferees, it may be a little trickier. They inherit either the employees or the dismissal liability. There may well be arguments about whether dividing the employment contract worsens working conditions. Some transferees may want to take the employees on, whereas others may not. Can one transferee's proposal to move job location effectively scupper the transfer to all transferees, even it does not affect the totality of the employee's work?

If employment terminates, it seems implicit from *Govaerts* that each transferee's liability for dismissal costs would be calculated based on the proportion of the employee's remuneration that they inherited (or would have inherited), after the split of contracts. But again, the CJEU's judgment is tantalisingly light on detail.

A complex web of competing interests quickly emerges, for which *Govaerts* provides no clear answers. Meanwhile, the employee is potentially left in no-man's land as the argument carries on around them (which is hardly consistent with safeguarding workers' rights).

Having said that, the employee also has the option to initiate termination. For some individuals, a portfolio of part-time employment contracts with different employers may well be an unattractive proposition (even if it could be arranged in practice). In those cases, Regulation 4(9) seems the most obvious avenue of redress.

Provided they have at least two years' service, this gives the employee with the right to resign and claim unfair dismissal, in response to a substantial change to working conditions to their material detriment[9]. Under *Govaerts*, even if division of the contract is possible, the contract can be terminated if it would lead to a worsening of working conditions. There is unlikely to much difference between these tests (and, even if there is, it would seem relatively straightforward to adopt a purposive interpretation of Regulation 4(9), to reflect *Govaerts*).

9 See **Chapter 8**

McTear: Service provision changes

Before *McTear*, the legal position regarding fragmentation in relation to service provision changes was relatively clear.

In *Kimberley Group Housing Ltd v. Hambley and ors*[10], the EAT determined that an assigned employee (and all the rights and liabilities associated with their employment) should transfer to the transferee which took on the majority of the work. As we have seen, this approach was rejected in *Govaerts,* in relation to the transfer of an economic entity. In *McTear*, the EAT confirmed that the *Govaerts* principle should apply equally to service provision changes. So *Kimberley* is no longer good law.

The facts in *McTear* were similar to *Govaerts*. A contract to provide replacement kitchens in council housing was re-tendered and split into two lots (north and south), which were awarded to two new contractors. The outgoing contractor allocated staff to each lot, based on where they had worked over the previous 12 months.

The EAT ruled that, in line with *Govaerts*, the employees' contracts should be split between the two new providers. The employment tribunal's decision (which was pre-*Govaerts* and applied *Kimberley*) was overturned. The EAT said that although there was no strict requirement to apply *Govaerts* to SPCs, it would be undesirable to have a different approach, depending on whether the transfer fell within Regulation 3(1)(a) or (b).

However, there are significant difficulties with this approach. Whilst it may not be ideal, the transfer of an economic entity and an SPC are concepts based on separate regimes. As we have seen in **Chapters 2 and 3**, they apply different tests and have been interpreted by mutually exclusive lines of case law, with the CJEU jurisprudence having little bearing on the SPC regime.

---

10 [2008] IRLR 682 (EAT)

There are some circumstances where a change in contractor could fall into both categories. In those instances, it makes sense that *Govaerts* should apply, on the basis that there is a transfer of an economic entity under Regulation 3(1)(a). But the case is less compelling if it is a service provision change only, under Regulation 3(1)(b).

Before *Govaerts* and *McTear*, it was well-established that if a service provision change resulted in complete fragmentation, there is no transfer at all[11]. This is likely to remain the case. If it can be said that, because of the way the activities have been distributed amongst two or more new providers, they are no longer fundamentally the same, the *Govaerts* principle is not engaged.

Practical issues

Finding a sensible solution to the conundrum of dividing contracts will, in practice, require the co-operation and buy-in of multiple parties.

In an ideal scenario, the parties would look to agree precisely how the contract should be divided up – which days and hours each employee spends working for each transferee. This will not always be straightforward, particularly where the transferees will have no direct contractual relationship (and perhaps no obvious incentive to co-operate with each other).

We have already seen how the competing commercial interests and operational priorities of the transferor, various transferees and (in an SPC re-tendering scenario) the customer may conflict. Roadblocks may emerge where, for example:

- two (or more) transferees are direct competitors. The employee will owe contractual confidentiality obligations, whether express or implied, in identical terms to each transferee – but it creates practical tensions. It is unlikely that each employer would

[11] *Clearsprings Management Ltd v. Ankers and anor* UKEAT/0054/08 (EAT)

ordinarily be comfortable with the commercial risk of its employees working for a competitor, whilst retaining access to its own IT systems or workplaces. How is this real or perceived threat managed in practice, without some direct contractual reassurance between the relevant employers?

Incidentally, the EAT in *Kimberley* had rejected the idea of splitting the employment contract between transferees, stating that it was against the established common law principle that an employee could not be the servant of two masters at the same time (especially if they were in competition).

- there is transfer of part of the undertaking only, resulting in the employment contract being divided between transferor and transferee (rather than two or more transferees). The employee may not to spend part of their week working for the transferee, in which case the transferee is responsible for any termination costs. But they are still left with reduced hours with the transferor, which in itself may cause them a substantial disadvantage. Can they rely on Regulation 4(9) as against the transferor, in those circumstances? And what happens if the situation is reversed – that is, the employee is willing to work for the transferee but not the transferor?

- employees are required to carry out duties at different locations at various times of the week. Additional travel time and costs may, of themselves, cause a *"worsening of working conditions"* under *Govaerts*. Even if the change in workplace would ordinarily fall within an existing contractual mobility clause and/or the relevant employers were willing to cover the extra commuting costs, such issues will likely require careful management.

- one or more of the new service providers decides to sub-contract part of the services (which could, in itself, cause further fragmentation and deepen the complexities caused by *Govaerts* and *McTear*).

Assuming there is some negotiated consensus, this would then need to be considered with appropriate employee representatives, as part of the TUPE consultation process. This is dealt with in **Chapter 17**.

CHAPTER ELEVEN

TRADE UNIONS AND COLLECTIVE AGREEMENTS

A unionised workforce can cause some complications in the context of a TUPE transfer, particularly if the transferee has limited experience of dealing with unions or collective agreements.

The laws around trade union recognition, collective bargaining and industrial action are labyrinthine (even compared to TUPE!) and potentially daunting for employers and practitioners unfamiliar with the various technicalities and procedural requirements. A detailed explanation of these is far beyond the scope of this text.

Similarly, there are potentially knotty issues where a process for union recognition or a ballot for industrial action straddles the transfer. Questions may arise, for example, in relation to the validity or continuation of such process as regards the transferee, who will not have been party to any previous recognition negotiations or caught up in the relevant pre-transfer dispute. Given that such instances are likely to be relatively rare in practice, I do not consider them in detail here.

Leaving that aside, the impact of a transfer on trade union relationships and collectively agreed employment terms can be summarised relatively succinctly.

Key principles

Under TUPE:

- a collective agreement which applies to a transferring employee shall continue to have effect as between the relevant union and the transferee (and anything done pre-transfer by the transferor shall be deemed to have been done by the transferee);

- if a trade union is recognised for transferring employees in an organised grouping of resources or employees which remains distinct from the rest of the transferee's business post-transfer, the transferee shall be deemed to recognise that union to the same extent;

- there is no transfer of rights and liabilities relating to collectively agreed terms which are agreed post-transfer, if the transferee is not a party to the collective agreement; and

- the transferee can vary collectively agreed terms because of the transfer, if the variation takes effect more than one year after the transfer and the employee's contractual terms are no less favourable overall.

These are considered in more detail below.

Trade unions may also play an important role in the pre-transfer information and consultation process. This is considered in **Chapter 17**.

Transfer of collective agreements

Regulation 5 states that where, at the time of the transfer, there is a collective agreement made by or on behalf of the transferor with a trade union recognised by the transferor in respect of any transferring employee:

> *"that agreement, in its application in relation to the employee, shall, after the transfer, have effect as if made by or on behalf of the transferee with that trade union, and accordingly anything done under or in connection with it, in its application in relation to the employee, by or in relation to the transferor before the transfer, shall,*

after the transfer, be deemed to have been done by or in relation to the transferee."

This is subject to a limited exception in ss.179 and 180 TULR(C)A (where collective agreements are presumed to be unenforceable in specified circumstances).

It is a straightforward principle, which incorporates Article 3(3) of the ARD and has needed no material judicial interpretation.

Provided that the relevant statutory definitions are met – namely, that there is a "trade union"[1] which is "recognised"[2] by the transferor and a "collective agreement"[3] in place at the time of the transfer which applies to the transferring employee – Regulation 5 will apply.

Collective agreements follow the transferring employees and are inherited by the transferee, in the same way as the individual contract of employment. Similarly, an order made in relation to that collective agreement (for example by the Central Arbitration Committee) will also have effect after the transfer[4].

Trade union recognition

TUPE provides for limited continuation of trade union recognition by the transferee post-transfer. Under Regulation 6(1), this only applies where *"the transferred organised grouping of resources or employees maintains an identity distinct from the remainder of the transferee's undertaking"*.

This is subtly different to the corresponding provision in Article 6(1) of the ARD, which requires the undertaking to have *"preserved its*

1 As defined in s.1 TULR(C)A

2 As defined in s.178(2) TULR(C)A

3 As defined in s.178(1) and (3) TULR(C)A

4 Regulation 5(b)

autonomy". The practical effect is likely to be the same. The ECJ has confirmed that "autonomy" means *"the right to self-government"* – such that the organisational powers of the transferred economic entity to give orders and instructions, allocate tasks and use the entity's assets in the pursuit of its economic activity are preserved within the transferee's broader organisational structure[5].

It appears from this that a decision by the transferee to integrate or amalgamate the transferring business into its existing operations will have the effect of shutting out a trade union that had previously been able to bargain collectively on behalf of some or all the transferring employees. They would need to go through the process of requesting recognition or seeking compulsory recognition to re-assert their influence, albeit the relevant bargaining unit and thresholds for compulsory recognition may need to take account of the transferee's wider workforce.

Otherwise, assuming the Regulation 6(1) test is met, an independent trade union recognised to any extent by the transferor in relation to any transferring employees shall be deemed to have been recognised by the transferee, to the same extent[6]. The union's remit will be exactly what it was pre-transfer – it will not apply to a wider category of employees, nor will it have the power to bargain collectively in relation to a broader range of issues.

Post-transfer collective bargaining

Regulation 4A states that TUPE:

> *"does not transfer any rights, powers, duties and liabilities in relation to any provision of a collective agreement if the following conditions are met:*

---

[5] *Federación de Servicios Públicos de la UGT v. Ayunamiento de la Línea de la Concepción and ors* C-151/09, [2010] ICR 1248 (ECJ)

[6] Regulation 6(2)

(a) the provision of the collective agreement is agreed after the date of the transfer; and

(b) the transferee is not a participant in collective bargaining for that provision."

This straightforward legal principle was the culmination of a protracted judicial debate, which reached the UK Supreme Court and was then referred to the CJEU.

In *Alemo-Herron and ors v. Parkwood Leisure Ltd*[7], Parkwood inherited employees following a transfer in 2004. Their contracts stated that their terms and conditions (including pay) were to be determined in accordance with a collective agreement with the relevant trade union, the NJC. The question arose as to whether Parkwood was bound by pay increases agreed with the NJC in subsequent years, where it was not a party to the pay negotiations.

At its heart was a tussle between two competing philosophies.

The "static" approach dictated that a transferee could only be bound by collectively agreed terms that were in force as at the transfer date. This appeared to be the ECJ's preferred method, albeit previous case law was on different facts and dealt with the peculiarities of German employment law[8].

Conversely, the "dynamic" approach stipulated that the transferee should continue to be bound by any terms negotiated with trade unions under a collective agreement after the transfer, even though it had no involvement in those discussions. This interpretation had previously been endorsed at appellate level in the UK[9].

---

7 [2011] IRLR 696 (UKSC)

8 *Werhof v. Freeway Traffic Systems GmbH & Co. KG* C-499/04, [2006] IRLR 400 (ECJ)

9 *Whent and ors v. T Cartledge Ltd* [1997] IRLR 153 (EAT)

In *Alemo-Herron*, the UK Supreme Court concluded that there was nothing to suggest TUPE was intended to adopt the more generous "dynamic" approach. However, it asked the CJEU to clarify the correct legal interpretation.

The CJEU determined that the static approach was correct and that the ARD:

> *"must be interpreted as precluding a Member State from providing, in the event of a transfer of an undertaking, that dynamic clauses referring to collective agreements negotiated and adopted after the date of transfer are enforceable against the transferee, where that transferee does not have the possibility of participating in the negotiation process of such collective agreements concluded after the date of the transfer"*[10]

This is surely correct and in line with the emerging trend (also confirmed by the CJEU in *Alemo-Herron*) that there must be a fair balance between the interests of the transferee and the transferring employees[11]. There is an obvious inequity in an employer being shut out from pay discussions with a trade union (at which one of their competitors may be present) but then bound by whatever is agreed in their absence.

Arguably, the CJEU has subsequently watered down its view in *Asklepios Kliniken Langen-Seiligenstadt GmbH v. Felja*[12], in which it did not rule out the "dynamic" approach in all circumstances. However, by then the "static" approach had been enshrined in Regulation 4A.

---

10 *Alemo-Herron*, C-426/11 [2013] IRLR 744 (CJEU), paragraph 37

11 *Alemo-Herron* (CJEU), paragraph 29

12 C-680 & 681/15, [2017] IRLR 653 (CJEU)

Variation of collectively agreed terms

Regulation 4(5B) states that a purported contractual variation, made for the sole or principal reason of the transfer, will not be automatically void if:

> "(a) *the variation of the contract takes effect on a date more than one year after the date of the transfer; and*
>
> (b) *following that variation, the rights and obligations in the employee's contract, when considered together, are no less favourable to the employee than those which applied immediately before the variation."*

At first glance, this one-year rule appears to be a significant curtailment of the default protection for employees against contractual changes (considered in detail in **Chapter 9**).

In particular, proposed variations to terms that do not derive from a collective agreement will not be saved by the one-year backstop provision in Regulation 4(5B)(a). They will have no effect if they are made because of the transfer, albeit the causal link between the variation and the transfer may weaken over time. We have already seen that, in one case, a proposed variation made two years after the transfer was considered void on such grounds[13].

However, this may give false confidence to employers seeking to wait out a year before disapplying collectively agreed terms for transferring employees (and perhaps bring them in line with what is offered to the rest of its workforce). There is still the requirement to ensure that the employee's terms are no less favourable overall.

An employer that takes away with one hand must give back with the other. A qualitative assessment of whether, for example, departing from

[13] *London Metropolitan University v. Sackur and ors* UKEAT/0286/06 (EAT) – discussed in **Chapter 8**

a collectively bargained pay scale or meal allowance but offering other benefits in return will inevitably be fact-sensitive.

The courts have not, as yet, been asked to offer any real guidance on this issue. The BIS Guide is also less than insightful:

> *"the employer could seek to agree effective variations to terms and conditions incorporated from a collective agreement which may result in those particular terms being less favourable to the employee provided that the employee gets some other more favourable terms so that overall the employee is in a no less favourable position after the variation compared to immediately before it."*

A parallel could potentially be drawn with the statutory regime relating to fixed-term employees. Specifically, less favourable treatment of a fixed-term employee can be justified on objective grounds (and is therefore permissible) if the terms of their contract *"taken as a whole, are at least as favourable as the terms of the comparable permanent employee's contract of employment"*[14].

However, this still has its difficulties. First, there is a similar paucity of judicial guidance on this principle as it relates to fixed-term employees, even though it has been in force for 20 years. Secondly, under TUPE, there is no comparator employee – it is simply a comparison between the employee's circumstances before and after the variation.

More generally, it is unclear how any comparison of the pre- and post-variation contractual terms should be undertaken. Should an objective approach be taken to the financial value of the benefit offered (assuming that can be calculated sensibly), or should the focus be on the relative subjective value for any given employee, depending on their personal circumstances?

---

[14] Regulation 4(1) of the Fixed-Term Employees (Prevention of Less Favourable Treatment) Regulations 2002

CHAPTER TWELVE

PENSIONS

The treatment of pension benefits as part of a TUPE transfer will, in many cases, be straightforward. If a transferee is entitled to or eligible for membership of a group personal pension scheme administered by a third-party provider (which seems to be the most common approach in practice), this right will simply be preserved by TUPE.

However, where the transferor operates an occupational pension scheme (or "**OPS**"), the landscape is significantly more complicated – both in relation to liabilities under the OPS and the requirement for transferees to put in place replacement pension benefits, post-transfer.

Key principles

The approach to pension rights under TUPE can be summarised as follows:

- if the transferor operates an OPS, any benefits relating to old age, invalidity or survivors <u>will not</u> transfer. However, the transferee has a statutory obligation to provide a minimum level of pension entitlement to transferring employees who were eligible for the transferor's OPS;

- any benefits under an OPS which do <u>not</u> relate to old age, invalidity or survivors <u>will</u> transfer to the transferee; and

- any obligation on the transferor to make pension contributions to a pension plan that is <u>not</u> an OPS will transfer in the normal way.

Occupational pension schemes

The first question to determine is whether or not the relevant pension arrangement is an OPS.

Under Regulation 10(1)(a), "occupational pension scheme" has the meaning given to it in the Pension Schemes Act 1993, where it is defined as:

> *"any scheme or arrangement which is comprised in one or more instruments or agreements and which has, or is capable of having effect in relation to one or more descriptions of categories of employments so as to provide benefits, in the form of pensions or otherwise, payable on termination of service, or on death or retirement, to or in respect of earners with qualifying service in an employment of any such description or category."*[1]

This is about as broad as it gets. There is perhaps a more useful steer in Article 3(4) of the ARD, which refers to *"supplementary company or intercompany pension schemes outside the statutory social security schemes in Member States"*.

In simple terms, an OPS refers to a pension scheme operated by the employer itself. Typically, it will be run by pension trustees appointed under a trust set up by the employer. Compare this to a scheme managed by an external pension provider, which invests contributions on the employee's behalf with the objective of growing their pension pot.

Many private sector employers will offer defined contribution pension benefits as part of a group personal pension scheme run by an institutional provider. In some instances (particularly for senior individuals), they may simply pay into a personal pension plan that the employee has already set up. These will fall outside the definition of an OPS. Any obligation on the transferor to make employer pension

1 s.1 Pension Schemes Act 1993

contributions to such schemes will simply transfer to the transferee, under Regulation 4(2). If the employer's contribution is contingent on the employee making a minimum contribution, this will be preserved.

Some private sector (and many public sector) employers will, however, continue to operate an OPS.

The remainder of this chapter focuses on the particular complexities relating to the treatment of OPS benefits, in the context of a TUPE transfer.

What transfers?

Under Regulation 10(1), TUPE does not apply to transfer any rights, powers, duties or liabilities relating to an OPS.

However, Regulation 10(2) states that:

> *"any provisions of an occupational pension scheme which do not relate to benefits for old age, invalidity or survivors shall be treated as not being part of the scheme."*

In other words, old age, invalidity and survivors' benefits do not transfer. This transposes the requirements of Article 3(4)(a) of the ARD. The employee retains any accrued rights in the transferor's OPS, up to the date of transfer – but the transferor remains liable for these.

Any other type of benefit under an OPS does still transfer.

This can cause heightened degrees of agitation for employment lawyers advising transferees, for good reason. It can potentially expose the transferee to significant liability under an OPS, which is not easy to quantify. As a result, the parties may seek to negotiate complex indemnity provisions or price adjustment mechanisms, which aim to mitigate or apportion such liability.

In particular, an acceleration of pension benefits that pays out before the employee's normal retirement age under the OPS may become the transferee's responsibility. This could be expensive and potentially arise several years after the transfer takes place.

There are three leading cases which illustrate the jeopardy for transferees:

- in *Beckmann v Dynamco Whichloe Macfarlane Ltd*[2], the ECJ held that enhanced redundancy payments and early retirement benefits triggered by redundancy under a public sector (NHS) occupational pension scheme fell clearly outside the scope of *"old age, invalidity or survivors' benefits"* under Article 3(4) of the ARD. They could not be considered to relate to "old age", as this only covered *"benefits paid from the time when an employee reaches the end of his normal working life"*[3]. Accordingly such benefits transferred to the transferee;

- in *Martin and ors v. South Bank University*[4], the ECJ endorsed *Beckmann* and adopted a similar approach to early retirement benefits (outside a redundancy scenario) and benefits intended to enhance the conditions of such retirement, again in the public sector; and

- in *The Proctor & Gamble Company and ors v. Svenska Cellulosa Aktiebolaget SCA and anor*[5], the *Beckmann* principle was applied in a private sector context by the English High Court. It did not matter that enhanced early retirement benefits were contingent on employer consent (in circumstances where the employee merely had a right to apply for them, rather than a right to be given them). Those rights could still transfer. However, any

---

2 C-164/00, [2002] IRLR 578 (ECJ)

3 *Beckmann*, paragraph 30

4 C-4/01, [2004] IRLR 74 (ECJ)

5 [2012] IRLR 733 (Ch)

retirement benefit paid after normal retirement age did not transfer, as it related to "old age".

These cases demonstrate a consistently narrow approach to what is considered old age, invalidity or survivors' benefits. It is also worth noting that any discretion afforded to the transferee to reject an employee's request for early retirement benefits under an OPS will not be unfettered. The employee will have an *"expectation of being fairly treated"*, in accordance with an implied duty of good faith which is specific to pension arrangements[6].

Post-transfer pensions protection

If the transferor is the employer for the purposes of an OPS, separate pensions legislation requires the transferee to provide transferring employees with a minimum level of pension benefit, post-transfer[7].

This is intended to go some way to replacing the loss of old age, invalidity and survivors' benefits under the OPS, although there is no obligation on the transferee to provide an equivalent level of pension provision, as long as it makes available a pension arrangement which complies with the minimum statutory requirements.

This post-transfer protection applies not only to transferring employees who were active members of the transferor's OPS immediately before the transfer, but those who were eligible to become members (even if they had not yet exercised their right to membership) and those who are not yet eligible but may be in the future.

If the transferor's OPS was a money purchase (that is, defined contribution) scheme, the protection only applies if the transferor was required to make employer's pension contributions[8].

---

6 *Proctor & Gamble*, paragraphs 70 and 75. This is known as the "*Imperial* duty", after the case authority which established it.

7 s.257(1) Pensions Act 2004

Assuming this is the case, it becomes a condition of the employee's contract of employment that the transferee must either:

- provide access to an OPS (which is either a defined benefit or money purchase scheme) run by the transferee[9]; or
- make contributions to a stakeholder pension scheme[10].

The minimum level of benefits to be provided will depend on the type of scheme the transferee chooses to offer.

For a money purchase or stakeholder OPS, the transferee must make employer pension contributions to match contributions the employee is required to make, up to 6% of basic gross pay. There is a proviso that if the transferor previously made employer contributions under a money purchase OPS, the transferee need not contribute more than the transferor did[11].

For a scheme which is not a money purchase scheme (such as a defined benefit scheme), the transferee can adopt the same approach outlined above. Alternatively, it has the option of ensuring that the scheme provides for the employee to be entitled to benefits valued at not less than 6% of pensionable pay for each year of employment (including the total amount of employee contributions), provided that if employees are required to contribute, their contribution should not more than 6% of

---

8 s.257(2) to (4) Pensions Act 2004

9 s.258(2) Pensions Act 2004

10 s.258(3) Pensions Act 2004. Note that from 1 October 2012, there was no longer a requirement for employees to offer access to a stakeholder pension scheme (a type of defined contribution scheme), although some employers may still operate a stakeholder scheme within the context of the pensions auto-enrolment regime.

11 Regulation 3 of the Transfer of Employment (Pension Protection) Regulations 2005

pensionable pay. "Pensionable pay" is defined by reference to the scheme rules[12].

If a transferring employee has not yet completed the requisite period of service before joining the transferor's OPS, they must do so before becoming eligible for the relevant post-transfer pension arrangements.

The transferee will, of course, also need to ensure that its new arrangements also comply with the minimum auto-enrolment obligations established by the Pensions Act 2008.

The introduction of new pension arrangements will likely constitute a "measure" that triggers an obligation to consult with employee representatives, in accordance with Regulation 13. These issues are considered in more detail in **Chapter 17**.

Separately, it may also be necessary for the transferor and/or transferee to engage in consultation under the Occupational and Personal Pension Schemes (Consultation by Employers and Miscellaneous Amendments) Regulations 2006. This legislation imposes a minimum 60-day consultation period where certain "listed changes" are proposed to an OPS or personal pension scheme, with potential fines for non-compliance. This topic is outside the scope of this book. It may be possible to combine a TUPE and pensions consultation into one process which satisfies (at least to some extent) the minimum requirements of both regimes.

Finally, under Regulation 10(3), a transferring employee cannot bring a claim for breach of contract or constructive unfair dismissal, if the transfer results in a loss or reduction of their rights under the transferor's OPS. Although it is not clear, this is also likely to preclude a

---

12 Regulation 2 of the Transfer of Employment (Pension Protection) Regulations 2005

claim under Regulation 4(9) (dismissal due to a substantial change in working conditions to the employee's material detriment)[13].

Practical approach

The question of whether the transferor has an OPS should be right at the top of any initial list of due diligence questions. Although it does not crop up that often in practice (particularly in the private sector), where it is relevant and deemed a material risk, it can have a potentially significant financial impact.

In particular, transferees should scrutinise the precise terms of the OPS and flush out anything which is potentially payable (or available) to employees before normal retirement age. As noted above, the transferee will inherit responsibility for any liabilities not related to old age, invalidity or survivors' benefits.

Further individualised data may be required to determine the potential value of such benefits, although this will likely require expert actuarial analysis. This can be useful for commercial arrangements such as those in *Proctor & Gamble*, where there was a contractual mechanism for reducing the purchase price to reflect the value of transferring pension liabilities.

The alternative approach is simply to negotiate a specific, targeted indemnity provision to deal with any future liabilities that may arise. These so-called "Beckmann indemnities" have the advantage of kicking down the road a problem that may never arise – and removing an otherwise potentially knotty commercial negotiation over price (which may also need to balance other risk factors, unrelated to employees). However, they can leave the paying party open to uncertain levels of liability over an unspecified period. This could be a step too far for the wary transferor, unless liability is capped or time-limited or there is an agreement to apportion the cost between the parties.

---

13 See **Chapter 8**

The other reason for needing clear information about any OPS at an early stage is that the transferee will need to establish whether it has to put in place alternative pension arrangements. It may already have an existing pension scheme which complies with the minimum requirements set out above, thus allowing it to harmonise pension arrangements relatively easily. Otherwise, it will need to make an early decision about what type of scheme to offer and explore the associated costs.

CHAPTER THIRTEEN

INSOLVENCY

When companies get into financial difficulties, the opportunity may arise to rescue some or all of the business as a going concern. A buyer may be found for the assets and the proceeds of sale can be used to repay creditors and cover an insolvency practitioner's fees. This can result in a TUPE transfer, with employees assigned to the relevant organised grouping of resources (and associated liabilities) transferring to the buyer.

TUPE recognises that to encourage buyers to rescue struggling businesses and preserve jobs, some of the usual protections for employees should be modified or disapplied in insolvency situations. This mirrors the flexibility in the ARD for individual member states to allow some employment debts to be covered by the state (rather than inherited by the transferee) and/or for agreed changes to terms of employment to be implemented by the transferee, where they are aimed at business survival.

Key principles

The application of TUPE to insolvency scenarios can be summarised as follows:

- If the insolvency proceedings are terminal (that is, they are instituted with a view to liquidating the assets of the transferor), the rules relating to the automatic transfer of rights and liabilities and TUPE-related automatic unfair dismissals do not apply.

- If the insolvency proceedings are not terminal, TUPE applies in the normal way, subject to a few modifications. First, the transferee does not inherit liability for certain payments guaranteed by the state. Second, it can make limited variations to a transferring employee's contract of employment, where they are aimed at ensuring the survival of the business.

TUPE does not refer specifically to "terminal" and "non-terminal" insolvencies – but the distinction is used as short-hand in practice. The boundary between them is not always entirely clear. This is because TUPE adopts the precise terminology used in the ARD, which does not fit neatly with the various categories of insolvency procedure under domestic legislation.

Terminal insolvency proceedings

Regulation 8(7) states that:

> *"Regulations 4 [Effect of relevant transfer on contracts of employment] and 7 [Dismissal of employee because of relevant transfer] do not apply to any relevant transfer where the transferor is the subject of bankruptcy proceedings or any analogous insolvency proceedings which have been instituted with a view to the liquidation of the assets of the transferor and are under the supervision of an insolvency practitioner."*

There is no confirmed list of which UK insolvency procedures will fall within this definition. In 2006, the Government issued "Redundancy and Insolvency Payments" guidance[1] (**"2006 Insolvency Guidance"**) which confirmed how it would treat various types of insolvency under TUPE, when determining who is responsible for redundancy payments. This categorises bankruptcy, compulsory liquidation and creditors' voluntary liquidation as falling within Regulation 8(7). The Government conceded that the 2006 Insolvency Guidance was *"not an*

---

1 BIS Guidance Document: *The Transfer of Undertakings (Protection of Employment Regulations) 2006 – Redundancy and Insolvency Payments* (archived on 9 June 2009)

authoritative interpretation" of TUPE (which only tribunals and courts can give). However, it is difficult to envisage how a court could determine otherwise, given their nature and purpose. As such, the 2006 Insolvency Guidance is a useful starting point.

Where an insolvency procedure falls within Regulation 8(7), the rules are relatively simple. Even if there is an economic entity which retains its identity or (much less likely) a service provision change, the employees will not transfer to the putative transferee (and have no claim for automatic unfair dismissal arising from TUPE). If the buyer of any assets chooses to take on an individual previously employed by the insolvent seller, there is no restriction on its ability to change terms and conditions (although continuity of employment will be preserved[2]).

Assuming that the insolvent employer is unable to meet its liabilities in relation to any impacted employees whose employment has been terminated, certain minimum amounts are guaranteed by the state through the National Insurance Fund (or "**NIF**"). In summary, these include statutory redundancy pay[3] and each of the following:

- up to 8 weeks' arrears of pay;
- up to 6 weeks' holiday pay;
- statutory minimum notice pay;
- a basic award for unfair dismissal; and

---

2 Under s.218(2) ERA 1996 – see *Oakland v. Wellswood (Yorkshire) Ltd* [2010] IRLR 82 (CA)

3 s.166 ERA 1996 – although note that under s.122(4) ERA 1996, any basic award for unfair dismissal is reduced by any statutory redundancy payment made

- reasonable reimbursement of any fee paid by an apprentice or articled clerk[4].

In each case, the amount payable is limited to the statutory cap of a "week's pay"[5]. From 6 April 2022, this was set at £571 per week[6], although it tends to increase in April each year.

The NIF would also normally cover certain unpaid contributions to occupational or personal pension schemes[7]. It appears that such debts could still transfer to the transferee[8], although only where the exception for occupational pension scheme liabilities under Regulation 10 does not apply.

Notably, Regulation 8(7) only operates to disapply Regulations 4 and 7. An impacted employee may still have a claim for ordinary unfair dismissal against the transferor (assuming a fair process was not followed). This may be of limited benefit, as they will likely rank as an unsecured creditor in relation to any compensation awarded by a Tribunal which is not covered by the NIF (and may therefore only recover a small fraction of the sum owed).

Potential buyers should be aware that there is also a technical risk that they may be held liable for failure to inform and consult under TUPE[9], for which they are unlikely to receive any indemnity protection from the transferor or an insolvency practitioner.

---

4 s.184(1) ERA 1996

5 s.186 ERA 1996

6 The Employment Rights (Increase of Limits) Order 2022

7 s.124 Pension Schemes Act 1993

8 Under Regulation 8(4), it appears that only debts covered by the NIF under ERA 1996 (and not the Pension Schemes Act 1993) would be excluded from transfer to the transferee

9 See **Chapter 17**

Non-terminal insolvency proceedings

Different rules apply if the transferor is subject to "relevant insolvency proceedings". These are defined in Regulation 8(6) as:

> *"insolvency proceedings which have been opened in relation to the transferor <u>not</u> with a view to the liquidation of the assets of the transferor and which are under the supervision of an insolvency practitioner."* (emphasis added)

The 2006 Insolvency Guidance categorised administration, voluntary arrangements and administrative receivership as "relevant insolvency proceedings". The Court of Appeal has since confirmed that administrations (including pre-pack arrangements), will always be "relevant insolvency proceedings"[10].

In these circumstances the normal TUPE rules apply, with two notable exceptions:

(1) <u>Some employment debts do not transfer</u>

Under Regulation 8(5), the transferee is not responsible for paying any sums which are otherwise covered by the NIF (see above).

This rule applies both to: (a) any employees whose contract of employment transfers under TUPE; and (b) anyone who is automatically unfairly dismissed before the transfer, under Regulation 7(1)[11]. However, it appears to exclude anyone who is dismissed but has less than two years' service, as such employees do not have unfair dismissal protection (whether under Regulation 7(1) or otherwise).

10 *Key2Law (Surrey) LLP v. De'Antiquis and anor* [2011] IRLR 272 (CA)

11 Regulation 8(2)

Importantly, any debts arising after the transfer (for example, where they arise from a dismissal by the transferee) are not covered by the NIF[12].

Similarly, any sums owing to employees which exceed or otherwise fall outside the remit of the NIF will transfer as normal.

(2) <u>Some contractual variations are permitted</u>

Regulation 9(1) states that:

> *"If at the time of a relevant transfer the transferor is subject to relevant insolvency proceedings these Regulations shall not prevent the transferor or transferee (or an insolvency practitioner) and appropriate representatives of assigned employees agreeing to permitted variations."*

A "permitted variation" means a change to the employment contract which: (a) is designed to safeguard employment opportunities by ensuring the survival of the business; and (b) would otherwise be void because the sole or principal reason is the transfer and there is no ETO reason[13]. This suggests that if there is an ETO reason, Regulation 9 does not apply at all.

The objective of safeguarding employment opportunities may, at first glance, appear to provide a broader licence to transferees to make changes, beyond the relatively stringent constraints of demonstrating an ETO reason. However, the underlying objective of ensuring the survival of the business may present a high bar.

A transferee brave enough to rely on it will need to address its mind (either at board or some other appropriate senior management level) to how the proposed variations would achieve that aim. Some contemporaneous evidence of the relevant business rationale in the

---

12 *Pressure Coolers Ltd v. Molloy and ors* [2011] IRLR 630 (EAT)

13 Regulation 9(7)

form of a written memo (or, at least, minutes of internal discussions) is recommended – and will, in any event, likely be required when presenting any proposals to representatives.

Importantly, a permitted variation can only be agreed with *"appropriate representatives of the assigned employees"*. This means there is no scope for the employer to agree changes to employment terms directly with individual employees. Equally, there is nothing to prevent an employer from agreeing bespoke changes to certain individual employment contracts, provided this is done through the appropriate representatives.

Trade union representatives must be treated as the *"appropriate representatives"* of assigned employees for which the relevant trade union is recognised[14].

If (and only if) there is no recognised trade union, assigned employees can either elect representatives specifically to discuss permitted variations or use the same representatives who were elected under Regulation 14 for the purposes of the TUPE information and consultation process[15]. However, in either case, they must have specific authority to agree permitted variations on behalf of assigned employees.

Further, where non-trade union representatives are in place, additional safeguards are in place requiring: (a) any permitted variation to be in writing and signed by each representative (or a duly authorised agent); and (b) copies to be provided to each employee to whom it will apply (prior to signature), together with any guidance they might reasonably require to understand it fully[16]. This suggests that any permitted variations require unanimous approval by the representatives.

Permitted variations can only be agreed in relation to employees assigned to the organised grouping of resources or employees that is the subject of the transfer. The issue of assignment is considered in detail in

---

14 Regulation 9(2)(a)

15 Regulation 9(2)(b)

16 Regulation 9(5)

Chapter 6. It excludes any of the transferor's employees who are not in scope to transfer. Similarly, any employees of the transferee who might be impacted by the arrival of assigned employees are not covered.

Unhelpfully, TUPE is silent on the timing of any agreement to the proposed changes. As set out in Regulation 9(1), the only requirement is that the transferor is subject to relevant insolvency proceedings *"at the time of a relevant transfer"*.

There is nothing to prevent the transferee seeking to agree permitted variations after the transfer, once it has had an opportunity to understand how the business operates and diagnose the reasons for its previous struggles. Clearly, this does not present an open-ended opportunity to the transferee to rely on Regulation 9 long into the future. Any such changes would still need to get through the appropriate representatives and as time elapses, it will likely become harder to demonstrate a causal link between varying contracts and ensuring the survival of the business.

If an individual assigned employee is unhappy with the variation agreed on their behalf by their representative, it appears that they have limited recourse to a remedy under TUPE. Regulation 9(6) expressly states that a permitted variation takes effect as a term or condition of the individual employment contract. This negates an argument that any contractual change is void under Regulation 4(4). It also appears to prevent the employee from relying on it in support of a claim for unfair dismissal, unless they can show that it is not designed to safeguard employment opportunities.

As an alternative, they might seek to argue that the variation was made for an ETO reason, therefore bringing it outside Regulation 9. Although this would not render the change void, it may allow the employee to resign and rely on Regulation 4(9), on the basis that it amounts to a substantial change to their material detriment[17].

---

17 See **Chapter 8**

Otherwise, Regulation 4(9) provides no remedy, as it is expressly subject to Regulation 9.

Other types of proceedings

For completeness, the 2006 Insolvency Guidance considered that members' voluntary liquidation and receiverships (other than administrative receiverships) were not insolvency proceedings at all. If correct, this would mean that Regulations 8 and 9 are simply not engaged for these types of action. However, as far as I am aware, this assumption has not received any judicial consideration.

CHAPTER FOURTEEN

BONUSES, INCENTIVES AND BENEFITS

We have seen already that most rights and obligations pertaining to transferring employees will transfer automatically to the new employer[1], with limited scope to change them simply because the transfer has taken place[2].

The transferee inherits what is in the contract and has to make do with it.

However, it is not always easy to put that principle into practice. Taken literally, the transferee may be required to replicate entitlements or incentives that are unique to the transferor – and which simply do not translate to the transferee's business.

For example, unless there is an intra-group transfer, a transferee cannot award shares or honour options over shares in the transferor (or the transferor's parent entity). It may be difficult to replicate bonus arrangements that are dependent on the financial performance of the transferor or certain areas of its business, where the transferee has a different operating structure or financial model. The transferee may offer different benefits through different providers.

The courts have grappled with these issues over many years, but not always with satisfactory results.

---

1 See **Chapter 7**

2 See **Chapter 9**

Bonus schemes

Where the transferor operates a bonus or other cash-based incentive arrangement, there are three questions for the transferee to consider:

1. Does the bonus scheme form part of (or is it connected with) the employee's contract of employment, such that the rights and liabilities relating to it transfer under TUPE?

2. If yes, can the transferee continue to operate the bonus scheme in its existing form, after the transfer takes place?

3. If that is not possible, what replacement bonus arrangements should be put in place?

Let's look at each of those issues in turn.

(1) *Contractual status*

Some contracts will provide a very clear entitlement to a bonus, provided certain conditions are met (for example, in relation to performance targets being hit and the employee remaining employed at the payment date). The right to receive a bonus in those circumstances will transfer in the normal way.

Other bonus arrangements are more vague or nuanced. For example, the contract may state that an employee is "eligible" to be considered for a bonus, with no further information on how such eligibility is assessed or any bonus calculated. In such cases, the transferee will still inherit the obligation to consider the employee for a bonus.

Similarly, a bonus scheme which is silent on whether it is contractual (or which has not been committed to writing) but has paid out consistently over a period of time may be implied into the contract as a matter of custom and practice (and therefore transfer under TUPE).

The position in relation to a non-contractual bonus is less clear. On one straightforward analysis, if it is expressly stated as not forming part of the employment contract, this should be sufficient to bring it outside the scope of TUPE. Even if bonuses have been paid historically, any scope for an implied contractual right should be trumped by the express clause confirming its non-contractual status.

However, the automatic transfer principle spreads its tentacles beyond what is strictly contractual. Regulation 4(2) states that "*all the transferor's rights, powers, duties or liabilities under or <u>in connection with</u> any such contract shall be transferred*" (emphasis added). A non-contractual bonus is likely to be connected to the employment contract, but does it give rise to a right, power, duty or liability?

We have some guidance from a case relating to discretionary early retirement benefits under a pension scheme. In *The Proctor & Gamble Company and ors v. Svenska Cellulosa Aktiebolaget SCA and anor*[3], the High Court determined that:

> *"the phrase 'rights and obligations' in Article 3(1) and in TUPE is to be liberally interpreted without regard to domestic distinctions between a discretionary entitlement and a legally enforceable right. The entitlement of the transferring employees, and its concomitant obligation, though discretionary, are such as to transfer by operation of TUPE accordingly."*

Although it is not completely on point, a court might reasonably adopt a similar purposive interpretation in the context of an expressly non-contractual bonus or benefit, to bring it within the scope of TUPE. This is the safest assumption to make. However, there may still be room to argue a distinction between an employee having an entitlement subject to the employer's discretion (as in *Proctor & Gamble*) and having no entitlement whatsoever.

Even if a non-contractual bonus does not transfer, a failure to offer the opportunity for similar earning potential (whether in the form of bonuses or otherwise) could still give the employee scope to resign and

3 [2012] IRLR 733 (Ch)

claim unfair dismissal, under Regulation 4(9)[4]. It would also likely be a "measure" requiring consultation under Regulation 13(6)[5].

(2) Maintaining the transferor's bonus scheme

If it is possible for the transferee to continue operating the transferor's contractual bonus scheme in the same way, then TUPE requires that it should do so. Under Regulation 4(2), the transferor's duties and liabilities in relation to such scheme are transferred to the transferee.

This may be perfectly achievable where, for example, the bonus is based on hitting individual performance objectives that can be ported across. It may also be possible to preserve a bonus scheme based on team targets (where the team has simply been dragged and dropped into the transferee's business and continues to operate in the same way). This will need to be assessed on a case-by-case basis.

Where a bonus award is otherwise stated to be discretionary, the transferee will still need to exercise its discretion rationally and show its workings. In doing so, it may be risky to depart from the transferor's previous approach in awarding or calculating any bonus payment, even if the transferee might otherwise have interpreted the scope of any discretion differently.

Should the transferee wish to alter the existing bonus scheme, it could rely on an existing variation clause (if any), in accordance with Regulation 4(5)(b). For example, many employment contracts will state that the employer has the express right to amend, withdraw, replace or discontinue a bonus scheme. However, once again, this will require consultation and the spectre of Regulation 4(9) looms large where any proposed replacement scheme is less favourable (or if there will be no replacement scheme at all).

---

4 See **Chapter 8**

5 See **Chapter 17**

(3) *Replacement bonus arrangements*

Where a bonus is determined, wholly or partly, by company performance or other criteria that are unique to the transferor's business (such as individual sales targets relating to the transferor's products or the share price of the transferor's parent entity), the position is more complicated.

Taken literally, TUPE requires the transferee to honour these bonus arrangements, even though they are not pertinent to the transferee's business (and beyond its control).

Regulation 4(2) demands that the transferee maintains the same terms and conditions of employment. So how can this very clear legal requirement be reconciled with the practical difficulties of replicating the transferor's bonus scheme?

This issue was considered in *Mitie Managed Services Ltd v. French and ors*[6]. The transferor (Sainsbury's) operated a profit-sharing scheme. It allocated part of its pre-tax sales profit to an employees' profit fund, using a set formula based on the group's sales and profit. From that profit fund, eligible employees were entitled to receive either a cash payment or an award of shares in Sainsbury's (such shares to be held on trust by Sainsbury's for three years).

The transferee (Mitie) did not – and clearly, could not – continue to operate the Sainsbury's scheme, even though the transferring employees had a contractual entitlement to participate. It had no access to the confidential information required to do so, nor did it have any power to issue shares in Sainsbury's.

Nevertheless, the EAT determined that transferring employees were entitled to:

6 [2002] IRLR 521 (EAT)

> *"participation in a scheme of substantial equivalence but one which is free from unjust, absurd or impossible features. In most cases, we would expect the transferee company to be able to negotiate a scheme of such equivalence with the transferred employees or their unions. If a negotiated conclusion is impossible, then it is appropriate for an application to be made to an Employment Tribunal, probably under section 11 of the Employment Rights Act, for a determination of the relevant particulars of employment."*[7]

The EAT conceded that it had not been easy, but considered that such an approach was consistent with the purpose of TUPE and the ARD *"to protect workers and, more particularly, to safeguard their rights upon a change of employer"*.

And yet, this is far from satisfactory for transferees. There is no guidance on what amounts to *"substantial equivalence"*, when the starting premise is that the original bonus scheme cannot be replicated.

We can take the facts in *Mitie* as an example. Even leaving aside the impossibility of awarding shares in the transferor, how could the transferee create a profit fund based on its own financial performance that provided a substantially equivalent opportunity for an employee to earn the same bonus that they would have received at Sainsbury's? In a different scenario, what if the employees had transferred to a small business with a mere fraction of the profits or revenue of Sainsbury's, such that it was not financially viable to operate a similar scheme? It is fraught with practical pitfalls.

There are also legal difficulties, particularly given developments since *Mitie* was decided in 2002. The EAT's suggestion that a new scheme could be negotiated with the transferring employees or their unions is inconsistent with the legislation. There is simply no scope under TUPE to agree a variation to terms and conditions on this basis, unless either: (a) there is an ETO reason (and Regulation 4(5)(a) is engaged); or (b) it

---

[7] *Mitie*, paragraph 16

falls within the scope of existing collective bargaining arrangements (under Regulation 5B).

An ETO reason is difficult to establish, as it requires a change to the numbers or job functions of employees (or the place of work), none of which will apply if the transferee is simply introducing different bonus arrangements. A variation agreed with unions under Regulation 5B can only take effect a year after the transfer.

It is also problematic in the context of the EAT's decision in *Ferguson and ors v. Astrea Asset Management Limited*[8]. This confirmed that a change to terms and conditions is void if it is introduced because of the TUPE transfer and there is no ETO reason, regardless of whether it is more favourable to the employee.

The only sensible advice that can be given to transferees in these circumstances is that they should do the best they can.

They should conduct as much due diligence as possible about the data underpinning bonus calculations and awards made in previous years. This has practical constraints, as many transferors will be reluctant give anything more than minimum employee liability information under Regulation 10, unless they are contractually obliged to.

They should document the efforts made to understand how the transferor's bonus arrangements operate and the precise steps taken to ensure, so far as possible, that any replacement scheme replicates the employees' previous entitlement such that it can be seen as "substantially equivalent".

If there is a tangible risk that employees will be worse off despite the transferee's best efforts (and may bring claims for higher bonuses calculated in accordance with the transferor's scheme), early consideration should be given to mitigating this risk through indemnity provisions or otherwise reflecting it in the commercial terms of the deal.

8 [2020] IRLR 577 (EAT) – discussed in more detail in **Chapter 9**

This may also be useful if a dissatisfied employee asks an employment tribunal to determine what the correct terms should be[9] – by protecting the transferee from any financial exposure arising from the tribunal's interpretation of what is substantially equivalent.

Share options and share incentives

The position in relation to share options and other share-based incentives also leads into treacherous waters. There is a myriad of share schemes that an employer may offer, from standard tax-efficient Enterprise Management Incentive (EMI), Save As You Earn (SAYE) and Company Share Option Plan (CSOP) schemes to very sophisticated share arrangements with complicated structures.

A transferee cannot honour an obligation in relation to share options in the transferor or its parent, nor can it grant or require the buy-back of shares in another entity. This is plain from the decision in *Mitie*.

The precise rules of the relevant scheme, the contracting parties and the degree of connection with the employment contract will all be relevant in determining how the employee's entitlement should be treated.

In particular, it is important to distinguish between any existing options or shares granted to the employee and any entitlement to receive future option grants or shares.

The employee may already hold shares or share options (whether vested and unvested). These will typically be handled in accordance with the rules of the relevant scheme, which will dictate how they are to be treated once the employee is no longer employed within the transferor's group. A transfer under TUPE may therefore trigger the relevant leaver provisions, with no obligation passing to the transferee at all.

9 See ss.11-12 ERA 1996. Note that an employer can also make this type of application, but it will rarely be in its interests to do so, in this context.

In relation to any promise of future awards, it is first necessary to consider whether it might transfer at all. As we have seen above, Regulation 4(2)(a) covers rights and liabilities *"in connection with"* the employment contract, which extends the automatic transfer principle beyond purely contractual terms. The fact that the scheme is expressed to be non-contractual may not be enough to sidestep TUPE.

Similarly, there is limited scope to argue that rights under a share scheme do not transfer because any entitlement arises not from the employment contract but from a separate contractual arrangement. In *Ponticelli (UK) Ltd v. Gallagher*[10], there was no mention of share incentives in the employment contract. However, a share incentive plan entered into between an employee and the transferor employer (under which shares were purchased in the transferor's parent company) was still deemed to be *"in connection with"* the employment contract.

Interestingly, a different approach may apply if the employee contracts directly with a group entity other than their employer. In *Chapman and anor v. CPS Computer Systems plc*[11], the Court of Appeal held that a share option agreement between the employee and the transferor's parent entity fell outside TUPE, because it was separate to the employment contract. *Ponticelli* decided the issue of separate contracts differently, noting the criticism levelled at *Chapman* by commentators because it did not specifically consider whether rights and liabilities under the CPS option contract were *"in connection with"* the employment contract. The EAT in *Ponticelli* decided to skirt around the (more senior) Court of Appeal's decision in *Chapman* by distinguishing it, on grounds that it related to a share option scheme, not a share incentive plan.

Perhaps it could have done so on the basis that *Chapman* concerned a contract with another group entity, not the transferor itself. When viewed through this prism, the outcome in *Chapman* seems consistent with the legislation. Regulation 4(2)(a) is concerned very specifically

10 [2022] EAT 140 (EAT)

11 [1987] IRLR 462 (CA)

with the transfer of the transferor's rights, powers, duties and liabilities – and not those of any other entity (whether in the transferor's group or otherwise).

If the transferee does inherit an obligation to offer future share options or other share-based incentives, the "substantial equivalence" test in *Mitie* will apply (notwithstanding its inherent difficulties).

As the transferee has no powers in relation to the transferor's share option scheme, it may have to offer the employee access to its own scheme, or establish a new scheme with similar rules to the transferor's scheme. This could cause all sorts of complications in determining substantial equivalence relating to, amongst other things, vesting conditions. It may require the transferee to alter any existing scheme rules or create options that may dilute existing shareholdings. The transferee may have to offer share options (and therefore, the future opportunity to own a stake in the business) to transferring employees when similar incentives are not available to its existing staff.

Equally, the transferee will also inherit the transferor's rights under any scheme (not just its obligations). If the transferor had the right to cease operating the scheme at any time, it seems reasonable that this would form part of a substantially equivalent scheme. This could then enable the transferee to walk away from any future obligations (although not, perhaps, from any unfair dismissal liability under Regulation 4(9)). As far as I am aware, this point has yet to be considered by the courts.

The transferee should also check whether there is an effective "Micklefield clause"[12] in the relevant employment contracts, which excludes liability in relation to the loss of share options or share awards arising from the termination of employment.

12 See *Micklefield v. SAC Technology Ltd* [1990] IRLR 218 (Ch)

Benefits and perks

The principles outlined above in relation to bonuses are likely to apply in a similar way to other benefits offered to transferring employees.

Many employers will provide insurance-backed benefits such as private medical cover, permanent health insurance (or "PHI") and life insurance, but not always in the same way. Others will use a wider array of perks to retain staff, such as cycle-to-work schemes, discounted gym membership, annual health screenings, staff discounts on company products, season ticket loans, long-service awards, an extra day's holiday on the employee's birthday, a Christmas hamper etc. The list is almost endless.

As such, it is relatively common to see a mismatch in employee benefits, as between the transferor and transferee. For example, one or both parties may offer a menu of different options from which an employee can choose, under a flex-benefits arrangement. The transferee may offer the same types of benefit as the transferor, but with different levels of entitlement or eligibility requirements. It may use different third-party pension providers or insurers to facilitate or administer those benefits.

Even if they are not strictly contractual, they may still be deemed "in connection with" the employment contract, requiring the transferee to honour them or offer something substantially equivalent.

A well-drafted employment contract should be clear that the employer is entitled to modify, withdraw or replace any benefit arrangements, change providers or even remove insurance cover for a particular employee if it is disproportionately expensive. This should allow the transferee to harmonise benefits arrangements or bring them under the umbrella of their existing providers by virtue of Regulation 4(5)(b), even if the sole or principal reason for doing so is the transfer itself.

In practice, very careful due diligence is required to ensure that the transferee understands fully what is currently on offer. The removal of a seemingly innocuous, low-cost benefit may cause a ruckus if it is cherished by employees, even if the transferee seeks to offer something ostensibly more valuable instead. This is where the TUPE information and consultation process can be especially useful, in flushing out and addressing such issues (and, in extreme cases, averting the risk of unfair dismissal claims under Regulation 4(9)).

Where the transferor offers PHI cover, the transferee should also check specifically that the relevant employment contract expressly permits the employer to terminate employment, even if the employee is in receipt of (or eligible for) PHI payments by virtue of their long-term sickness absence. This is important in avoiding potentially significant liability which might otherwise arise from the implied term not to dismiss, where the effect is to deprive the employee of PHI benefits[13].

---

13 *Aspden v. Webbs Poultry and Meat Group (Holdings) Ltd* [1996] IRLR 521 (QB)

CHAPTER FIFTEEN

RESTRICTIVE COVENANTS

We have seen in **Chapter 14** some of the complexities in applying the automatic transfer principle to certain entitlements or perks enjoyed by a transferring employee. Of course, the employment relationship is not all one-way traffic.

Regulation 4(2) refers explicitly to the transfer of the transferor's *"rights"* and *"powers"*, as well as its *"duties"* and *"liabilities"*. The transferee inherits the benefit as well as the burden of the employment contract.

For the most part, this is very straightforward. Most of the employee's express and implied contractual duties simply become owed directly to the transferee, at the point of transfer.

There is, however, one difficult exception. The enforceability of restrictive covenants in the employee's contract can present a particular problem for both transferors and transferees.

The basic, well-known principle is that a post-termination restriction will only be enforceable if it goes no further than is reasonably necessary to protect the employer's legitimate business interests (that is, its confidential information, client connections or workforce stability). But how does a transferee seek to enforce the benefit of post-termination restrictions that have been drafted for the purpose of protecting the transferor's business?

The *Morris Angel* principle

In *Morris Angel & Son Ltd v. Hollande and anor*[1], the Court of Appeal considered the enforceability of a restriction preventing the employee soliciting or dealing with customers, following a TUPE transfer. Specifically, the employment contract stated as follows:

> *"The Executive covenants with the Company that he will not for the period of one (1) year after ceasing to be employed under this Agreement (without the prior written consent of the Board) on his own behalf or on behalf of any person firm or company directly or indirectly seek to procure orders from or do business with any person firm or company who has at any time during the one (1) year immediately preceding such cesser done business with the Group ..." "directly or indirectly seek to procure orders from or do business with any person firm or company who has at any time during the one (1) year immediately preceding such cesser done business with the Group".*

A literal application of the automatic transfer principle suggests that when looking at the extent of the employee's obligation, you should simply scrub out the name of the old employer and insert the new employer in its place. So the "Company" means the transferee, not the transferor, who then benefits from the covenant in the same way (and to the same extent). The "Board" can mean the transferee's board of directors and the "Group" can refer to the transferee's group companies.

This was, in effect, the approach adopted by the High Court, but the Court of Appeal took a very different view:

> *"The difficulty about that approach to my mind is that it turns the obligation on the employee... into a quite different and possibly much wider obligation than the obligation which bound him before the transfer... Such an obligation was not remotely in contemplation when the services agreement was entered into and I can see no reason*

1 [1993] IRLR 169 (CA)

why the regulation should have sought to change the burden on the employee."[2]

The Court of Appeal determined that although the transferee could still seek to rely on the covenant, it only applied to customers of the *"undertaking transferred"* – that is, the specific business it inherited from the transferor. It could not be extended to apply to customers of the transferee more generally (who were not otherwise customers of the undertaking that had transferred). The ambit of the restriction was, in effect, frozen in time.

Although consistent with the widely-accepted judicial approach to construing restrictive covenants narrowly, this seems an illogical outcome. In many cases, covenants that are entirely enforceable by the transferor will be rendered entirely impotent in the hands of the transferee.

Regulation 4(2) is clear that the transferor's *"rights"* and *"powers"* are transferred to the transferee. There is no reason why this should not give the transferee a right to protect its own legitimate business interests and the power to enforce the covenants it inherits for its own benefit through court proceedings, if necessary. Had Parliament intended the benefit of restrictive covenants to fall outside this, it could have legislated for it in the same way as, for example, the occupational pension schemes exception under Regulation 10. It did not do so.

It would be straightforward for a court to treat a restrictive covenant as if the employee had contracted with the transferee from the outset, rather than the transferor. In line with well-established principles of interpretation, it could still assess the effectiveness of the restriction as at the time it was entered into (and not at the time the transferee sought to rely on it)[3]. This does not seem to be an unduly artificial approach.

---

2 *Morris Angel*, paragraph 23

3 *PatSystems Holdings Ltd v. Neilly* [2012] IRLR 979 (QB)

Surprisingly, the principle in *Morris Angel* has received very little further judicial scrutiny in the past 30 years. Recently, the High Court in *P14 Medical Ltd v. Mahon*[4] granted an injunction in favour of a transferee on the uncontroversial premise that TUPE transfers restrictive covenants in the same way as other terms and conditions. However, it was not required to consider the restrictive interpretation of covenants post-transfer.

Morris Angel does seem ripe for reconsideration. The Court of Appeal explicitly recognised that *"the protection of employee rights was the primary objective"* and a *"purposive construction"* to TUPE was required[5]. This is perhaps now outdated, particularly given the growing focus on maintaining a balance between the transferring employees' and the transferee's interests, rather than simply defaulting to the most favourable outcome for the employee[6].

Practical implications

The practical impact of *Morris Angel* can cause difficulties, particularly for transferees.

First, a transferring employee may, over time, obtain a deep knowledge of their new employer's trade secrets or develop strong working relationships with its existing major customers. Such information and connections would clearly be valuable to a competitor, or indeed to the employee themselves if they chose to set up their own business.

And yet, the transferee cannot rely on the restrictive covenants it has inherited, to protect such legitimate business interests.

---

4 [2021] IRLR 39 (QB)

5 *Morris Angel*, paragraph 21 – applying the principles set out in *Litster v Forth Dry Dock & Engineering Co Ltd* [1989] IRLR 161 (HL)

6 This is considered in **Chapter 9**, in the context of changing terms of employment

It may still be able to rely on an express confidential information clause to obtain a springboard injunction in certain cases, to prevent misuse of confidential information from creating an unfair commercial advantage. However, this is a narrower form of protection.

It also assumes that the *Morris Angel* principle does not apply to post-termination contractual confidentiality obligations – that is, by only protecting the confidential information of the *"undertaking transferred"*. I am not aware of any case law on this point but it seems unlikely. Unlike restrictive covenants, the law does not place any limits on the scope of an express confidentiality undertaking in an employment contract – so the concerns expressed by the Court of Appeal about such obligations becoming wider post-transfer has less resonance.

The second issue is that, having inherited an ineffectual restrictive covenant under TUPE, there is almost no scope for the transferee to vary it or introduce new, more enforceable restrictions. This would be void under Regulation 4(4), as it would amount to a variation because of the transfer[7]. There is also no sensible basis on which to argue that a desire to improve an employee's non-compete restriction amounts to an ETO reason. Therefore, the transferee may need to wait until it can show that the sole or principal reason for introducing new restrictions was not the transfer itself[8].

Thirdly, there is the conundrum of the enterprising employee who does not wish to transfer and, instead, lines up a role at a competitor. They can simply object to the transfer under Regulation 4(7) and bypass the restrictive covenants altogether. The transferee cannot enforce them, even in the narrow sense permitted by *Morris Angel.* The contract of employment is treated as terminated and never transfers to the transferee. The transferor may still be able to rely on the covenants, but

---

7 For an example of this, see *Credit Suisse First Boston (Europe) Ltd v. Lister* [1998] IRLR 700 (CA)

8 See **Chapter 9**

may no longer have any legitimate business interest (or may simply be disinterested) in doing so.

PART D

TUPE PROCESSES

CHAPTER SIXTEEN

EMPLOYEE LIABILITY INFORMATION

TUPE establishes a statutory regime that places a pre-transfer obligation on the transferor to disclose certain minimum information to the transferee about individuals who are (or would otherwise have been) in scope to transfer.

Article 3(2) of the ARD allows Member States to *"adopt appropriate measures to ensure the transferor notifies the transferee of all the rights and obligations which will be transferred"*. It is optional rather than mandatory and, in 2006, the UK decided to take up that option. Not all EU countries have done so.

In practice, the contracting parties to an outsourcing contract will often include provisions that place a far broader contractual obligation on the transferor to share more comprehensive details about in-scope employees, at a much earlier stage. The purchase of a business will often conduct a due diligence exercise, backed up by warranties and/or indemnities from the seller in the purchase agreement.

However, that is not always the case. Therefore, TUPE steps in to require a base level requirement of information-sharing. This does, at the very least, give the transferee some advance warning of any significant liabilities on the horizon or, for example, the potential mismatch of benefits or incentives – even if it has limited usefulness in changing the commercial dynamics of the relevant transaction.

This chapter considers the technical legal issues relating to the transferor's obligation to provide employee liability information (and the remedies available to a transferee for non-compliance). Practical considerations in relation to the disclosure of employee information more generally are covered in **Part E** of this book.

Key principles

Under Regulation 11:

1. The transferor is required to notify the transferee of certain "employee liability information" (commonly known as "ELI") relating to anyone assigned to the organised grouping of resources or employees that is subject to the transfer[1].

2. This includes former employees who would have been so assigned, had their employment not terminated in the circumstances set out in Regulation 7(1) – namely, where they are dismissed pre-transfer and the sole or principal reason is the transfer itself (and not an ETO reason)[2].

   A narrow interpretation of this would suggest that it only applies to those who qualify for protection from automatic unfair dismissal under Regulation 7(1), but I doubt this is the intention. Former employees with less than two years' service who might otherwise have transferred may still have other claims (such as discrimination) which will be inherited by the transferee. The spirit and purpose of Regulation 11 dictates that ELI should include details of all liabilities that may transfer, particularly when read alongside Article 3(2) of the ARD.

3. "Employee" has the wider definition given to it in Regulation 2(1) – and therefore could potentially include current or former "limb (b) workers"[3].

---

[1] Regulation 11(1)

[2] Regulation 11(4)

[3] See **Chapter 6** for a detailed discussion of this issue

4. The ELI must be provided at least 28 days before the transfer – or, if there are special circumstances, within a shorter *"reasonably practicable"* timeframe[4]. This is not a big window, but it is better than nothing (and pre-2014, it was 14 days!).

   The BIS Guide suggests that a shorter timeframe may be justifiable where *"the transferor did not know the identity of the new employer until very late in the process, as might occur when service contracts are re-assigned from one contractor to another by a client, or, more generally, when the transfer takes place at very short notice"*[5].

   The term *"special circumstances"* is also used (and very narrowly defined) as an exception to collective redundancy consultation obligations[6], but in that context it is not contingent on the transferor being aware of a potential new third-party employer. A more generous interpretation of *"special circumstances"* may apply for the purposes of Regulation 11 and it seems sensible not to penalise the transferor in such cases.

5. The ELI must be provided by the transferor either in writing or in another readily accessible form[7]. This could include, for example, sending electronic files or providing access to an online data room.

6. The ELI must contain information as at a specified date not more than 14 days before it is provided[8]. Any changes to that information must be notified to the transferee in writing. There

---

4 Regulation 11(6)

5 BIS Guide, page 34

6 s.188(7) TULR(C)A 1992

7 Regulation 11(1)

8 Regulation 11(3)

is no express requirement to provide information in another *"readily accessible form"* where ELI is being updated[9].

7. The ELI can also be given in more than one instalment and/or indirectly through a third party[10]. This allows the customer in a re-tendering process to act as a conduit for information, passing it from the outgoing service provider to the intended new employer. It also permits the drip-feeding of ELI, provided that the overall timeframes above are complied with.

What is employee liability information?

Under Regulation 11(2), ELI comprises the following in relation to each employee:

- identity and age;

- the particulars of employment required under s.1 ERA 1996. There is no broader requirement on the transferor to disclose the full terms of the employment contract, although it may choose to do this for administrative ease. If the information under s.1 ERA 1996 includes non-contractual benefits, these should be disclosed too (although there is no requirement to specify what is or is not contractual[11]). This aligns with the broader principle in Regulation 4(2) that rights and obligations *"in connection with"* the employment contract will transfer, even if they are not strictly contractual.

  In some cases, the transferor will want to do no more than give the bare minimum, perhaps in a simple spreadsheet (particularly if it does not wish to provide a competitor with additional information regarding its approach to employment terms);

9 Regulation 11(5)

10 Regulation 11(7)

11 *Born London Ltd v. Spire Production Services Ltd* [2017] IRLR 493 (EAT)

- information of any grievance or disciplinary procedure in the previous two years, where the ACAS Code of Practice on Disciplinary and Grievance Procedures applies. There is no guidance on the level of detail required, but it would appear to include circumstances where a grievance was not upheld or no disciplinary action was taken (note that Regulation 11(2) refers to disciplinary "procedure", not "sanction"). The correct approach may well be dictated by data protection requirements (see below);

- information of any court or tribunal case, claim or action either: (a) brought against the transferor in the previous two years; or (b) which the transferor has reasonable grounds to believe will be brought by the employee, arising out of their employment. Again, neither TUPE nor the BIS Guide specify the level of detail to be provided.

  In terms of whether a transferor has *"reasonable grounds to believe"* a claim will be brought, the BIS Guide simply states that it is a *"matter of judgment and depends on the characteristics of each case"*. It gives the example of an accident at work, comparing a *"trifling"* incident where an employee slipped but did not take time off to a situation where it led to a long period of hospitalisation or a union representative raised a health and safety concern[12]. Clearly, there will be many shades of grey in between. It is safest to assume that any intimation by an employee that they may pursue a claim should be taken seriously for these purposes; and

- information of any collective agreement that will have effect after the transfer under Regulation 5(a).

12 BIS Guide, page 34

Data protection

If personal data is being shared by the transferor in accordance with Regulation 11, it will have a lawful reason for doing so. Specifically, Article 6(1)(c) of the UK General Data Protection Regulation ("**UK GDPR**") permits processing which is *"necessary for compliance with a legal obligation to which the controller is subject"*.

This will not apply if information is being provided outside the strict confines of Regulation 11 – for example, where:

- there is a contractual obligation to disclose more than the minimum ELI, or the transferor voluntarily chooses to do so; and/or

- information is provided at a significantly earlier stage than Regulation 11 requires (for example, as part of a re-tendering process or in the general course of providing services). Given the requirement for the transferor to notify the transferee of ELI under Regulation 11, any situation in which a specific transferee has yet to be identified will likely require a more circumspect approach.

In those circumstances, the current employer should consider carefully its data protection obligations and take appropriate steps accordingly. This may include anonymising or pseudonymising data, or not disclosing certain information at all.

The Information Commissioner's Office has produced some helpful guidance to assist employers in complying with data protection obligations in the context of disclosing ELI. It is somewhat out of date and based on the previous regime under the (now repealed) Data Protection Act 1998, rather than the UK GDPR and Data Protection Act 2018. However, it is still a useful source for sense-checking the overall practical approach.

It reminds those involved in the process that, even in relation to minimum ELI, *"both parties must take care to comply with data protection principles when handling this personal information"*[13].

This will include, for example:

- data minimisation – the transferor should not send to the transferee more information than is necessary to comply with Regulation 11. This can be tricky to judge in relation to grievances, disciplinary issues and claims where, as noted above, there is no guidance on how much detail to disclose. Typically, transferors are well-advised to take a cautious approach and provide no more than a short summary of the relevant matter;

- fair processing – the transferor should consider whether the data subjects would have a reasonable expectation that such data is shared with the transferee for the purpose of complying with ELI obligations. This can be achieved through a well-drafted privacy notice, which should put employees on notice that their data may be shared as part of any future corporate activity; and

- appropriate security measures – this applies in relation to both the sharing of ELI itself and the storage and retention of such information by the transferor and the transferee, after the transfer has taken place.

Particular care should be taken when transferring personal data outside of the UK.

Remedies for non-compliance

If the transferor fails to comply with its obligations under Regulation 11, the transferee can seek a remedy in the Employment Tribunal, in accordance with Regulation 12.

---

13 ICO Guidance: *Disclosure of employee information under TUPE*

This will take the form of a declaration and the Tribunal *"may make an award of compensation to be paid by the transferor to the transferee"*[14]. In doing so, it will consider what is *"just and equitable in all the circumstances"*[15] and must have regard to:

- any loss suffered by the transferee attributable to non-compliance. Therefore, the principles of causation will be relevant. Similarly, the Tribunal will apply the normal common law rules relating to the transferee's duty to mitigate its loss[16]. In this respect, compensation for non-compliance with ELI obligations is approached differently to a financial award for failure to inform and consult with employee representatives under Regulation 15, which is punitive in nature; and

- any contractual terms between the transferor and transferee which already deal with the transferor's liability for failure to notify the transferee of ELI. This will not be relevant where a customer is moving services from one provider to another (as there is no direct contractual relationship between transferor and transferee).

Rather curiously, Regulation 12(5) provides for a minimum award of £500 per employee, unless the Tribunal considers it *"just and equitable, in all the circumstances, to award a lesser sum"*. So it is a minimum amount which is not actually a minimum, but more a starting point from which the Tribunal can go up or down as it sees fit.

Importantly, the award only applies to employees for whom ELI requirements have not been met[17]. If the transferee has full ELI for some employees which has been provided at least 28 days before the transfer, it cannot claim in respect of them.

---

[14] Regulation 12(3)

[15] Regulation 12(4)

[16] Regulation 12(6)

[17] Regulation 12(5)

Any claim must be brought within three months of the transfer. The Tribunal has the power to extend this where it is satisfied that it was *"not reasonably practicable"* for the claim to be presented within three months[18].

[18] Regulation 12(2)

CHAPTER SEVENTEEN

INFORMATION AND CONSULTATION OBLIGATIONS

TUPE imposes a duty on employers to provide information to (and, where measures are envisaged, consult with) employee representatives about a proposed transfer, in good time before it takes place.

The duty is wide-ranging and seen as a cornerstone of TUPE protection. Complying with it requires careful planning and navigation by HR, often in conjunction with other (non-employment) workstreams which flow from a planned commercial transaction.

It can have a significant impact on the overall timing of the project, particularly if employee representatives need to be elected and there are measures envisaged which require thorough and meaningful consultation. In multi-jurisdictional transactions, an information and consultation process in the UK may need to be dovetailed with those in other EU member states or countries with analogous protections, where the precise requirements and timeframes under local law may be different. This needs to be factored in from the outset.

The potential liability for non-compliance can be significant. The punitive nature of the available financial remedies acts as an incentive for employers to take their information and consultation obligations seriously. The rules are quite prescriptive so, although the parties will sometimes cut corners in the interests of commercial expediency, this carries some degree of risk. The prospect of joint and several liability promotes co-operation between the parties, often with the safety net of careful drafting in commercial agreements to provide indemnity protection for breaches which may be beyond one or other party's control.

Key principles

There are five principal elements to the duty to inform and consult:

1. Employee representatives: An employer must first identify appropriate employee representatives of affected employees, with whom to engage. Save in limited circumstances, informing and consulting with employees directly will amount to a breach of the relevant statutory requirements. However, some employers will choose to do so – for example, if a small number of employees are affected or where there is only a duty to inform (and no duty to consult).

2. Duty to inform: Once the employee representatives are in place, the employer must provide them with certain minimum information about the proposed transfer, such as the underlying reasons for it and the potential impact on affected employees.

3. Duty to consult: Where measures are envisaged in relation to affected employees, the employer must consult the employee representatives about such measures, with a view to reaching an agreement. If no measures are proposed, there is no duty to consult.

4. Pre-transfer collective redundancy consultation: If the transferee envisages potential redundancies after the transfer that could result in collective redundancy consultation obligations being triggered, there is the option (with the transferor's agreement) to commence that process alongside TUPE consultation, before the transfer takes place.

5. Compensation: Failure to comply with the duty to inform and consult can result in liability of up to 13 weeks' pay per employee (imposed jointly and severally on the transferor and

transferee). The seriousness of the breach will be relevant to the Employment Tribunal's assessment of the appropriate award. There is a limited "special circumstances" defence.

Outside the TUPE regime, an employer may also need to comply with any separate obligations it may have under the Information and Consultation of Employees Regulations 2004. Such considerations are beyond the scope of this book, but may arise where the employer has a pre-existing employee consultation body in place.

Employee representatives

Regulation 13 imposes a duty to inform (and, if measures are envisaged, consult with) *"appropriate representatives of any affected employees"*.

Appropriate representatives

If an independent trade union is recognised for some or all the affected employees, the employer must inform and consult with representatives from that union in relation to those employees[1]. There is no choice.

For employees who are not of a description in respect of which there is trade union recognition, the employer does have a choice. It can either inform and consult with:

- employees elected specifically for the purpose of TUPE information and consultation[2]. Regulation 14(1) sets out the relevant requirements for an election. They include a broad overarching obligation *"to make such arrangements as are reasonably practicable to ensure that the election is fair"*, together with more specific rules governing (for example) the appropriate number of representatives and their term of office; arrangements for secret voting and accurate counting of ballots; and ensuring

1 Regulation 13(3)(a)

2 Regulation 13(3)(b)(ii)

that affected employees are entitled to vote and not unreasonably excluded from standing as a candidate; or

- existing employee representatives who already have the requisite authority from the employees to engage in TUPE information and consultation on their behalf[3]. This could be, for example, an internal employee forum or staff council. However, employers should be cautious in ensuring that any existing employee body has the requisite mandate, before proceeding on this basis. If in doubt, it is usually better to hold elections.

Sometimes, a hybrid approach will be necessary – for example, by informing and consulting union representatives for employees in the relevant bargaining unit but electing representatives for those outside it.

In practice, any election of representatives will take some time – typically, at least a week to allow for nomination and, if necessary, election. For larger exercises, it may be helpful to use a third-party service to run the election process.

There are two exceptions to the general requirement to inform and consult employee representatives, rather than the affected employees themselves.

First, it does not apply to "micro-businesses" employing fewer than 10 employees in total, assuming that existing representatives are not already in place (whether through a trade union or otherwise). In those circumstances, the employer can choose whether to invite affected employees to elect representatives or treat each individual employee as if they were a representative (by liaising with them directly)[4].

Second, if the employees have been invited to elect representatives but fail to do so within a reasonable time, the employer can provide the

---

3 Regulation 13(3)(b)(i)

4 Regulation 13A

required information directly to the employees[5]. TUPE is silent on whether the employer can also consult directly regarding any measures, but it may have no option if there are no representatives to whom they can talk. This is likely to be better than no consultation at all.

In practice, some employers will choose to run the risk of providing the required TUPE information to all affected employees and, when doing so, ask them if they would prefer to elect representatives (rather than be informed and consulted directly). However, it is not without risk. Providing information to employees directly is in itself a breach of Regulation 13 requirements, even if representatives are subsequently elected and the same information is provided again, through those representatives.

Once elected, employee representatives have certain additional rights and protections. These include paid time off to perform their duties[6]; protection from detriment[7] and automatic unfair dismissal[8] for carrying out their duties; and access to appropriate accommodation and other facilities[9].

Affected employees

This extends far beyond those individuals who are envisaged to transfer from the transferor to the transferee. It includes:

---

5 Regulation 13(11)

6 s.61(1)(a) ERA 1996

7 s.47(1)(a) ERA 1996 – this protection also extends to candidates for election (s.47(1)(b) ERA 1996) and those participating in an election (s.47(1A) ERA 1996)

8 s.103(1)(a) ERA 1996 – again, this protection also extends to candidates for election (s.103(1)(b) ERA 1996) and those participating in an election (s.103(2) ERA 1996). The requirement for a minimum of two years' continuous service does not apply in such cases – s.108(3)(f) ERA 1996)

9 Regulation 13(8)

> *"any employees of the transferor or the transferee (whether or not assigned to the organised grouping of resources or employees that is the subject of a relevant transfer) who may be affected by the transfer, or may be affected by measures taken in connection with it..."*[10]

It will also cover, for example:

- anyone employed by the transferor who is not in scope to transfer and will therefore be left behind. Such individuals may need to be assigned alternative duties or potentially be placed at risk of redundancy, where some of their previous work has been transferred elsewhere. There may also be a wider knock-on effect on staff working in centralised functions (such as HR, IT or Finance) who will have fewer employees to support;

- employees who have pending internal applications for jobs in the transferring undertaking (but not everyone in the workforce who might apply in the future for a vacancy)[11];

- existing employees of the transferee who may become caught up in a post-transfer redundancy selection pool, because the arrival of transferring employees will cause an excess of resources or capacity within the business; and

- affected "limb (b) workers" who fall within the wider definition of employee in Regulation 2(1)[12]. This could include consultants engaged by either transferor or transferee, who are deemed surplus to requirements and may therefore have their contracts terminated.

---

10 Regulation 13(1)

11 *UNISON v. Somerset County Council and ors* [2010] IRLR 207 (EAT)

12 See **Chapter 6**

Duty to inform

Under Regulation 13(2) and 13(2A), the employer of affected employees must provide the following information to their representatives:

- the fact that the transfer is to take place, its date (or proposed date) and the reasons for it: This is a relatively straightforward requirement. There is little guidance on how much detail the employer must provide about the reasons for the transfer. As the duty to consult under TUPE does not extend to discussing the underlying business rationale for the transfer, a light-touch approach should be sufficient. However, the reasons given should, of course, be accurate and not selective with the truth[13];

- the *"legal, social and economic implications"* of the transfer for affected employees: This language is lifted straight from the ARD but, again, there is no guidance on what it means. An explanation of legal implications will likely require the employer to outline that transferring employees will go across on their existing terms and conditions of employment. Any economic or social implications may amount to "measures" in any event;

- any *"measures"* envisaged to be taken in relation to any affected employees in connection with the transfer: This will either be measures envisaged by the employer itself or, in the case of the transferor, any measures it is envisages that the transferee will take. The transferee is required to provide information to the transferor about its proposed measures, to enable the transferor to comply with its obligations to inform and consult with affected transferring employees[14].

---

13 See, for example, *LLDY Alexandra Ltd (formerly Loch Lomond Distillery Company Ltd) v. UNITE the Union and anor* UKEATS/0002/14 (EAT)

14 Regulation 13(4)

"Measures" is another term lifted from the ARD. It has been described as *"a word of the widest import [which] includes any action, step or arrangement"*[15]. In addition to proposals that may have a material impact on employees – such as post-transfer redundancies, changes to benefits or new shift rosters – this would suggest it can include what may appear to be relatively innocuous administrative issues, such as a slight alteration in pay date;

- <u>suitable information about agency workers</u>: This includes the number of agency workers working temporarily across the employer's business, the parts of the business in which they work and the type of work carried out. This requirement was added by the Agency Worker Regulations 2010, but it is unclear why it is necessary for affected employees to receive it. Information about the transferor's agency worker cohort is likely to be of little use to employees transferring out of that business. Equally, there is no requirement for the transferee to disclose information to transferring employees about its own agency workers (which arguably would be useful, if post-transfer redundancies might be under consideration).

Such information must be provided *"long enough before a relevant transfer to enable the employer of any affected employees to consult the appropriate representatives of any affected employees"*. This is unhelpfully vague.

In practice, the length of any consultation over measures (and therefore, the timeframe for providing information under Regulation 13(2)) will depend on the extent and potential impact of such measures on employees and the number of employees who are affected by them. Even where no measures are proposed, the employer cannot simply provide the required information at the last minute. Although the

15 *Todd v. Strain and ors* [2011] IRLR 11 (EAT) at paragraph 18, citing *Institution of Professional Civil Servants v Secretary of State for Defence* [1987] IRLR 373 (Ch)

statutory duty to consult under Regulation 13(6) does not strictly arise in such cases, the employer still needs to leave time for voluntary consultation or informal discussions that might be requested by employees or their representatives[16].

Duty to consult regarding measures

Regulation 13(6) states as follows:

> *"An employer of an affected employee who envisages that he will take measures in relation to an affected employee, in connection with the relevant transfer, shall consult the appropriate representatives of that employee with a view to seeking their agreement to the intended measures."*

As can be seen, the obligation to consult is on the employer that envisages taking measures. This is straightforward where the employer already employs the affected employees.

However, in relation to the transferring employees, it is the transferee (not the transferor) that will usually propose measures. It leads to a clunky mechanism whereby:

- the transferee is required to inform the transferor of any envisaged measures[17]; and
- the transferor has a duty to tell the affected transferring employees about such measures[18]; <u>but</u>
- technically, the transferor has no duty itself to consult with affected transferring employees (because they are the transferee's measures).

---

[16] *Cable Realisations Ltd v. GMB Northern* [2010] IRLR 42 (EAT)

[17] Regulation 13(4)

[18] Regulation 13(2)(d)

In practice, the transferor will sometimes allow the transferee access to representatives of the transferring employees, to enable them to discuss proposed measures directly (rather than simply hearing it second-hand from the transferor).

There is no specific minimum period for TUPE consultation (unlike, for example, the 30- or 45-day period that applies to a collective redundancy consultation process).

As noted above, the duration of consultation is driven by the requirement to provide information to representatives long enough before the transfer to enable consultation to take place. In relation to transferring employees, this may be dictated by when the transferee receives employee liability information (typically, at least 28 days before the transfer) so it can assess whether it envisages any measures.

For affected employees who are not transferring, there are no such parameters. Again, it may be difficult for a transferee to know whether there are measures which might affect their existing workforce until it sees the employee liability information (particularly if it is unsure how many employees might be transferring). A transferor is more likely to know at an earlier stage who is in scope to transfer and the potential impact of the transfer on employees who will be staying with them.

It is, of course, possible in theory to delay the transfer date if the consultation process takes longer than expected – although in many cases, that will likely have a knock-on effect on commercial arrangements and may therefore be unpalatable.

The key requirement is that consultation must be *"with a view to reaching an agreement"*. A prudent employer will set the wheels in motion, as soon as it becomes clear that potential measures are afoot in relation to its own employees. This will reduce the risk of allegations by employee representatives that consultation was perfunctory or otherwise not genuine.

After the transfer has taken place, there is no right or obligation to continue TUPE consultation[19]. This cuts both ways. An employer does not have the opportunity to rectify a defective or truncated consultation process by extending it post-transfer. Equally, there is no scope for employee representatives to continue debating or challenging proposed measures (and delay their implementation), by arguing that no agreement has yet been reached.

Where it is not reasonably practicable for the employer to comply with any aspect of the duty to inform or consult due to *"special circumstances"*, it must take all such steps towards its performance that are reasonably practicable in the circumstances[20]. In other words, if there are good reasons why the employer cannot comply fully, it must do the best it can.

As we have seen with the duty to provide employee liability information, the special circumstances defence is likely to be construed narrowly. The burden is on the employer to prove such special circumstances existed[21]. It cannot rely on a failure by another person which controls it (such as a parent company) as special circumstances[22].

The defence was accepted by the EAT in *UNISON v. Somerset County Council and ors*[23], where negotiations relating to an outsourcing of services by two local councils to a joint venture they had set up with IBM were *"proceeding at pace and the deadline for completing the agreement... was fast approaching"*. However, that decision needs to be seen in its particular context.

---

19 *Amicus and anor v. City Building (Glasgow) LLP and ors* [2009] IRLR 253 (EAT)

20 Regulation 13(9)

21 Regulation 15(2)

22 Regulation 13(6)

23 [2010] IRLR 207 (EAT)

There had been, in fact, what the EAT described as *"exemplary consultation"* over the previous two years, but the dispute arose in the context of some last-minute negotiations on one particular issue around the process for advertising future job vacancies. There was no consultation on these late changes, which the EAT concluded were not "measures" in any event. Even if they were, the Tribunal had been entitled to find that there were special circumstances where *"the situation in the negotiations was pressurised and that IBM were seeking to unpick the whole agreement which would have had disastrous consequences"*[24].

It is hard to know whether IBM walking away would truly have meant *"disastrous consequences"*, but this aspect of the decision should be treated with caution. I am not convinced that the anticipated collapse of a commercial outsourcing deal should, of itself, be considered special circumstances – except, perhaps, where the likely result was the potential insolvency of the transferor and/or mass redundancies.

More generally, *UNISON v. Somerset County Council* should not be relied upon as a green light to avoid consultation obligations because of the pressures of a self-imposed deadline.

Pre-transfer collective redundancy consultation

Under s.198A TULR(C)A 1992, the transferee has the option (but no obligation) to commence collective redundancy consultation with representatives of transferring employees who may be impacted by post-transfer redundancies, before the transfer takes place. This will arise where the transferee proposes to dismiss as redundant 20 or more employees at one establishment, within a 90-day period.

This process is distinct from TUPE consultation regarding measures, under Regulation 13. Failure to comply gives rise to a separate remedy for a protective award, which should not be conflated with

[24] *UNISON v. Somerset County Council,* paragraph 26

compensation for breach of TUPE consultation requirements. Therefore, the normal requirements for collective redundancy consultation will still need to be adhered to, subject to a few minor alterations as outlined in s.198B TULR(C)A.

Importantly, pre-transfer collective redundancy consultation can only take place with the consent of the transferor. This may not always be forthcoming, particularly if the transferor and transferee are competitors. It may also be contingent on the transferee providing indemnity protection for any claims.

In practice, it will also require the transferor's co-operation in providing appropriate access to representatives and otherwise not impeding the process. If this does not materialise, the transferee can cancel the process if it wishes[25] (and start again at a later date). It cannot, however, rely on the transferor being difficult to argue "special circumstances" for non-compliance with its collective redundancy consultation obligations[26].

In addition, the transferee will need to conduct individual redundancy consultation for transferring employees who have two or more years' continuous service.

Remedies for non-compliance

Where an Employment Tribunal finds that there has been a breach of information and consultation requirements (by either the transferor or the transferee), it:

- shall make a declaration to that effect; and
- may award *"appropriate compensation"* of such sum *"as the tribunal considers just and equitable having regard to the*

[25] s.198A(5) TULR(C)A 1992

[26] s.198B(1)(i) TULR(C)A 1992

seriousness of the failure of the employer to comply with his duty" – but capped at 13 weeks' pay per employee[27].

The approach to assessing any compensation is similar to that for failure to comply with collective redundancy consultation obligations under TULR(C)A – namely, the purpose of a compensation award is to punish the employer and act as a deterrent, not simply to make good any losses suffered by the employees[28].

Therefore, the starting point is to award the full 13 weeks' pay. However, the Tribunal does have a wide ambit of discretion in assessing compensation. An award can be reduced if there are mitigating circumstances which justify a lower amount. This may occur, for example, where some genuine efforts to inform and consult have been made, even if the employer's approach fell short of the standards required by Regulations 13 and 14[29].

Given the punitive approach to assessing financial awards and their significant exposure to liability in large-scale transfers, legal advisers should always flag the potential consequences of failure to comply, at an early stage. Sometimes, the liability for any failure to inform and consult will be apportioned between the parties using indemnities in the relevant commercial agreements.

Where there has been an alleged breach, the road to obtaining compensation is somewhat circuitous. It will typically work like this:

1. Bringing the claim: Where a trade union or other employee representatives are in place, they will typically need to pursue

---

27 Regulation 16(3)

28 *Sweetin v. Coral Racing* [2006] IRLR 252 (EAT) – which considered and applied the principles established by the Court of Appeal in the context of collective redundancy consultation in *Susie Radin v. GMB and ors* [2004] IRLR 400 (CA)

29 See, for example, *Todd v. Strain and ors* [2011] IRLR 11 (EAT) at paragraph 28, where an award of 7 weeks' pay per employee was upheld

litigation on behalf of the affected employees. An individual affected employee can only bring a claim in limited circumstances – for example, where there has been a failure relating to the election of representatives or those representatives do not have the necessary mandate[30]. The burden is on the employer to ensure that any representatives had the authority to represent the employees[31].

2. Identifying who is liable: A Tribunal will determine who is liable for any compensation as follows:

    a. If a complaint against the transferee is well-founded, it will order the transferee to pay compensation[32];

    b. If a complaint against the transferor is well-founded, it will order the transferor to pay compensation unless it can show that the failure is due to the transferee failing to provide measures information in good time (in which case, the transferee may be held liable)[33]. However, if the transferor wishes to pass the blame onto the transferee, it has to give the transferee notice of its intention to do so (which automatically makes the transferee a party to the proceedings)[34].

3. Enforcing a compensation award: Any order for compensation will be made in relation to *"such descriptions of affected employees who may be specified in the award"*. If an individual falls within any such category but does not receive compensation, they must

30 Regulation 15(1)

31 Regulation 15(3)

32 Regulation 15(7)

33 Regulation 15(8)

34 Regulation 15(5)

bring a separate complaint to the Tribunal (which can then make an order in relation to that individual)[35].

Any claims must be brought within three months of either: (a) the relevant transfer (in relation to 1. above); or (b) the date of the Tribunal's original order for compensation (in relation to 3. above), unless the Tribunal considers a longer period is reasonable because it was not reasonably practicable for the claim to be submitted within three months[36]. The clock can be stopped in the normal way, to allow time for ACAS early conciliation.[37]

Liability is joint and several as between the transferor and transferee, but only where: (a) an award is made against the transferor under Regulation 15(8)(a); or (b) either party fails to pay an award made against them and the Tribunal makes a further order following a claim brought by an individual under Regulation 15(11).

The Tribunal has no jurisdiction to apportion liability itself, based on its own assessment of the extent to which each party should be held responsible for any breaches. If there is a dispute between the transferor and transferee regarding who should be responsible for paying an award, this would need to be resolved through separate litigation in the courts, under the Civil Liability (Contribution) Act 1978.

Under Regulation 18, any claims for failure to inform and consult under TUPE cannot be waived by an individual under the terms of a settlement agreement.

An alternative approach is to discourage claims by requiring the employee to provide a warranty in a settlement agreement that it will not bring any such claims (and/or indemnify the employer in relation to any losses it incurs as a result of such claims). This may be seen as going against the spirit of Regulation 18 – and potentially contravenes

35 Regulation 15(10) and 15(11)

36 Regulation 15(12)

37 Regulation 15(13)

it (as arguably it excludes or limits the operation of TUPE) – although I am not aware of any cases that have considered it.

It is, however, possible for such claims to be settled under a COT3 agreement, conciliated through ACAS[38].

[38] Regulation 16(1)

PART E

TUPE IN PRACTICE

CHAPTER EIGHTEEN

NEGOTIATING COMMERCIAL AGREEMENTS

The parties involved in any given transaction cannot agree between themselves that TUPE will or will not apply.

However, they can (and frequently will) negotiate specific commercial terms to:

- agree practical steps to reduce the risk of TUPE applying (if that is the preferred outcome);
- override the default consequences of any TUPE transfer (namely, that most pre- and post-transfer employment liabilities rest with the transferee) by apportioning costs in a different way;
- provide an enhanced degree of control over who will be assigned to perform any work (and what the employer can or cannot do with them); and/or
- augment the statutory obligation to provide employee liability information obligation, both in relation to the scope and timing of that information and assurances regarding its accuracy.

TUPE clauses or schedules often cover many pages and can become unwieldy. This may reflect the complexity of the arrangements, an abundance of caution from one or other party or sometimes (dare I say it) the unrestrained pen of a verbose drafter. Brevity often aids clarity, but it is not always possible to achieve.

The adage that no two TUPE transactions are ever truly the same rings true, so I do not attempt to cover all possible permutations here. Instead, this chapter considers the most common types of transfer indemnity and other commercial provisions that may be negotiated between the parties.

Chapters 19 to 21 consider the specific issues that may arise in multi-jurisdictional projects and cross-border transfers, how to manage TUPE projects effectively and commercial considerations from the perspectives of each of the putative transferor, putative transferee and the customer moving services from one provider to another. They should be read in conjunction with this chapter.

Types of agreement

Although TUPE clauses can appear in a wide variety of commercial agreements, they will almost always fall into one of two buckets:

- transactional agreements – involving the sale or transfer of a business, commercial real estate, assets and/or goodwill from one entity to another – for example, under a business sale agreement; and
- services agreements – under which one entity outsources certain activities to another.

These agreements do not need to be between two unrelated entities. A hive-across of assets between two companies in the same corporate group or an arrangement whereby one subsidiary performs certain work on behalf of another and charges the costs back could equally fall within TUPE.

At the risk of over-simplification, transactional agreements are more straightforward in principle. There is usually a one-off sale or transfer event, to which TUPE may or may not apply. The commercial provisions will, in large part, comprise transfer indemnities focused on that specific event. A gradual or phased transfer of assets can complicate things, but ultimately an assessment will need to be made as to the precise point at which responsibility for the relevant undertaking is assumed by the transferee.[1]

In contrast, a services agreement usually requires a more comprehensive set of provisions. There will be at least two points in time when TUPE will need to be considered. Employees may move at the start of the arrangement (from customer or existing provider to the contracting provider) and at the end (from contracting provider to customer or replacement provider). There could be other transfers at intermediate stages – for example, if more services are added or some are removed during the term of the contract.

Transfer indemnities

The purpose of any transfer indemnities is to override the automatic transfer of most liabilities to the transferee, under TUPE.

The scope of such indemnities will depend on the commercial realities underpinning the relevant transaction – in particular, the relative bargaining strengths of the parties, their strategic priorities and whether they want (or anticipate) that TUPE will apply.

This will often dictate whether there is a "balanced" approach (whereby the parties apportion liabilities between them) or a "blanket" approach (under which one party accepts most or all the risk and costs of a TUPE transfer).

[1] See **Chapter 2** for a more detailed discussion of the timing of the transfer

Balanced approach

A useful starting point for a balanced set of transfer indemnities is that each party is responsible for what happens on its own watch. Neither party should be liable for acts or omissions of the other. Beyond that, there may be a commercial compromise between them to share costs on other matters (such as redundancies).

A balanced approach is more common where TUPE is envisaged to apply. The relevant agreement will often include a list of individuals whom the parties consider to be "transferring employees". This requires careful due diligence. An agreed list may not be definitive, as TUPE applies by operation of law. There may be others who do not make the list but who may still transfer (or allege that they transfer). These are sometimes known as "wrong pocket" or "woodwork" employees.

A standard balanced TUPE clause or schedule might then reflect the following:

- Pre-transfer liabilities: The transferor is responsible for costs and claims relating to the employment of transferring employees relating to events before the transfer. This may include some provision for specific costs, such as pre-transfer accrued holiday.

- Post-transfer liabilities: Similarly, the transferee is responsible for employment costs and claims relating to events after the transfer.

- Failure to inform and consult: The transferor is liable for any failure to comply with Regulations 13 and 14 in relation to transferring or wrong pocket employees, except where this arises because the transferee has not complied with its duty to provide measures information under Regulation 13(4).

- Regulation 4(9) and 4(11) dismissals: The transferee is responsible for any unfair dismissal claim by a transferring employee who resigns in response to a proposed substantial change to their terms and conditions to their material detriment, under Regulation 4(9). The transferor is responsible for any pre-transfer constructive dismissal which falls within Regulation 4(11), unless caused by the transferee.

- Redundancy costs: The transferor will pay (or make a partial contribution to) the termination costs of any transferring employees dismissed for redundancy by the transferee. This could be a percentage of overall costs or limited to specific types of payment (such notice or statutory redundancy pay). It will usually be time-limited and may be contingent on the transferee carrying out a fair redundancy process.

- Employee liability information: The transferee agrees that it will not bring any claim against the transferor for any inaccurate or incomplete information provided in relation to transferring employees (including any breach of Regulation 11). The transferee may be asked instead to stand behind the accuracy of its employee information, by providing appropriate warranties.

- Beckmann liabilities: The transferor will pay for any post-transfer liabilities arising from an occupational pension scheme that are not related to old age, invalidity or survivor's benefits[2].

- Wrong pocket mechanism: The transferor will pay for any post-transfer employment or termination costs relating to wrong pocket employees. However, it is unwise for a transferor to give an open-ended commitment, without some onus on the transferee to mitigate such costs. A typical approach is to require the transferee to notify the transferor of a claim by a wrong pocket employee and given them an opportunity to re-hire that person. If they do not do so, the transferee can then terminate employment within a limited timeframe.

---

2 See **Chapter 12**

This apportionment of responsibility is underpinned by carefully drafted cross-indemnities given by each party to the other.

There are, of course, innumerable variations on the above. Commercial negotiations on certain sticking points will often lead to creative solutions.

Blanket approach

If TUPE is not intended to apply or one party has a particularly strong hand, a blanket approach may be adopted instead. Indemnities are usually given by the putative transferor, as it is better-placed to control pre-transfer arrangements to minimise the risk of a TUPE transfer.

A typical clause might say:

- the parties do not envisage that TUPE will apply;
- the transferor warrants that no employees are assigned to an organised grouping of resources or employees on the transfer date (or would have been so assigned, but for their dismissal);
- however, if TUPE does (or is alleged to) apply to any individual, the transferor will indemnify the transferee for any costs or liabilities relating to the employment of such individuals or its termination.

Again, it would be sensible for the transferor to negotiate reasonable limits on its liability, by using a wrong pocket mechanism.

A blanket approach may also be agreed as a backstop where it is intended that in-scope employees will be offered enhanced redundancy terms under a pre-transfer tripartite settlement agreement (to which the transferee may contribute).

The lifecycle of the services contract

A well-drafted TUPE schedule in a services contract should cover three bases:

1. Entry: The potential transfer of employees to the service provider on commencement of services;

2. During the term: Controlling resourcing and employee information relating to the services, both generally and in the period before termination; and

3. Exit: The potential onward transfer of employees to a new provider on termination.

Entry

The agreement should include provisions in relation to any potential transfer of employees from either: (a) the customer itself, where activities are currently performed in-house and being outsourced for the first time; or (b) an incumbent service provider, where activities are currently outsourced and the customer is re-tendering those services.

The scope of any entry transfer indemnities may be influenced by any corresponding exit transfer indemnities in the existing contract between the customer and incumbent service provider. There will be no contractual nexus between the incumbent and new provider, although the new provider may have a right to enforce indemnity protection under the Contracts (Rights of Third Parties) Act 1999. The customer may wish to pass on the benefit of those indemnities to the new provider, but go no further.

It may also be necessary to agree the scope of any transitional arrangements, particularly in outsourcing arrangements.

During the term

Most commercial services agreements will contain general provisions which require the service provider to ensure that work is performed to a high standard by individuals with the requisite skills, training and experience. There may be a dedicated account manager or core cohort of key staff providing the services (although this can, in some cases, increase the risk of TUPE applying on exit). These provisions may sit outside the TUPE clause or schedule.

The customer may wish to reserve the right to "vet or veto" key staff – that is, to pre-approve individuals being introduced to the account or require the service provider to remove individuals from performing the services and offer a suitably-qualified replacement. Some customers require extensive background and criminal record checks to be undertaken for all individuals performing the services.

It is also reasonably standard to require the service provider to provide information (including terms and conditions of employment) regarding the employees performing the work, when requested by the customer. This will go beyond the confines of minimum employee liability information obligations under Regulation 11, both in relation to timing and detail. There are, however, data protection issues to consider[3] and the service provider may seek to limit the frequency of any requests. Typically, it is most useful when the customer is considering re-tendering or bringing the activities in-house, as it can assist potential bidders in pricing their services and/or getting a sense of potential termination costs.

Once a service provider is on notice that services may be re-tendered and/or the contract is being terminated, the contract may specify further controls on how the service provider can manage its workforce. These are known as "standstill" provisions. They may include restrictions on swapping employees on and off the account (or otherwise increasing or reducing the proportion of time spent by an

3 See **Chapter 16**

individual performing the work) and a prohibition on varying terms of employment (including awarding pay rises or bonuses). They are designed to guard against "poison pill" tactics, whereby the outgoing provider seeks to redeploy its most valued staff, off-load poor performers by assigning them to the transferring services or otherwise increase costs for the new, incoming provider.

<u>Exit</u>

Exit transfer indemnities will often be a mirror image of the entry transfer indemnities – so where a party gives an indemnity on commencement, it receives the benefit of an identical indemnity on termination (and vice versa).

The customer will normally want any indemnities from the service provider to be given for the benefit of both itself (in case it decides to bring the activities back in-house) and any replacement service provider that might win a contract for future services, following a re-tender process. This can be very useful protection to offer when negotiating commercial terms (including pricing) with any future service provider.

Some arrangements will provide the customer with significant control over who might transfer onwards. For example, it may wish to specify that the number of transferring employees is no more (and/or no fewer) than those who transferred in on entry. The agreement may state that only the precise individuals who transferred in (or those hired as their direct replacements) can transfer out on exit.

The contract might also include a contractual right for the customer (or a replacement service provider) to make an offer of employment to any employee providing the services who may not otherwise transfer under TUPE. This is less standard. In contrast, there may be a non-solicitation provision in favour of the service provider, throughout the term of the agreement.

Top tips: Giving and receiving indemnities

Giving an indemnity

- Do your due diligence. It is important to gather as much information as possible to assess potential exposure to liability.

- Define carefully what "liabilities" are covered. For example, if you are making a contribution to redundancy costs, what exactly does that include? Is it a percentage of overall costs, or simply an agreement to pay some or all of certain types of liability (such as notice pay or statutory redundancy pay). Is it contingent on the party making the redundancies following a fair process under section 98 ERA 1996 (or is this not relevant, because dismissals are likely to be automatically unfair under Regulation 7)? Do liabilities include legal costs?

- Keep control of those liabilities. Consider a time limit on claims (say, six months post-transfer), a cap on liability (a maximum amount covered) or a collar (a minimum amount not covered, akin to an excess under an insurance policy). Caps and collars can apply either cumulatively or in relation to an individual claim. Where litigation is threatened or commenced, consider reserving the right to assume conduct of proceedings, or at least the right to approve or reject a settlement offer.

- If you are passing on the benefit of an existing indemnity, ensure that what you are offering does not go beyond the protection you have. This is usually best achieved by copying across the indemnity, word-for-word.

Receiving an indemnity

- Ensure you are protected – will the indemnifying party be able to pay? In particular, be careful where there are complicated corporate group structures and seek a parent company guarantee if necessary.

- If the other party is unwilling to give a full indemnity, consider alternatives such as splitting liability or seeking a contractual warranty. Failing that, does the price or any other commercial term of the transaction or services need to be altered, to reflect any increased financial exposure?

- Some agreements may include a price adjustment mechanism, to cover unforeseen costs. However, this will need to be carefully drafted to define precisely what costs might be in scope and any duty to mitigate loss.

- Check whether any TUPE-related costs are covered by an overarching cap on liability or other form of control, hidden elsewhere in the agreement.

- Extend protection to third parties (including group companies, sub-contractors or a future replacement service provider) under the Contracts (Rights of Third Parties) Act 1999.

CHAPTER NINETEEN

INTERNATIONAL TRANSFERS

It is relatively common for potential transfer scenarios to occur in the context of multi-jurisdictional projects or cross-border transactions. These may include a decision by a UK business to outsource a support function to an overseas service provider, the re-tender of a global facilities management contract or an intra-group reorganisation implemented by a multi-national corporation.

This chapter considers when TUPE or similar legislation in other countries may be relevant to transactions involving more than one country and the practical and commercial consequences that may arise.

Transfers out of the UK

The application of TUPE will depend on where the organised grouping of resources or employees is based, immediately before the transfer. This should not be conflated with the issue of where any given assigned employee actually performs their work.

Where is the organised grouping of resources or employees situated?

For the transfer of an economic entity, the relevant undertaking, business or part thereof must be *"situated immediately before the transfer in the United Kingdom"*[1].

A service provision change requires that *"immediately before the service provision change… there is an organised grouping of employees situated in Great Britain"*[2].

[1] Regulation 3(1)(a)

In *Holis Metal Industries Ltd v. GMB and anor*[3], the EAT confirmed that: (a) the sale of assets by a UK company to a purchaser in Israel amounted to a transfer of an economic entity under Regulation 3(1)(a); and (b) the same approach could apply equally to an SPC. Any practical difficulties in enforcing rights under TUPE against an overseas transferee were irrelevant. As one of very few cases on cross-border transfers, the judgment in *Holis* is worth reading.

Therefore, the normal principles for determining whether there has been a transfer should be applied. We need to look at both the pre-transfer position and the proposed post-transfer arrangements:

- Pre-transfer: The location of employees overall will be relevant to whether there is a transfer of an economic entity and/or an SPC capable of triggering TUPE.

  Under Regulation 3(4)(c), the transfer of an economic entity can still occur where persons employed in the relevant business or undertaking ordinarily work outside the UK. If most or all of the assets comprising the relevant undertaking are situated in the UK, it may not matter that employees assigned to that undertaking work overseas. However, for a labour-intensive undertaking where most of the staff are overseas, there may be no organised grouping of resources in the UK (and therefore TUPE would not be triggered).[4]

  For a service provision change, if most or all of the employees are based overseas, there cannot be the necessary organised grouping of employees situated in Great Britain[5]. Although

2 Regulation 3(3)(a)(i) – note that the territorial scope for a service provision change is Great Britain, not the United Kingdom. SPCs in Northern Ireland are governed separately by The Service Provision Change (Protection of Employment) Regulations (Northern Ireland) 2006.

3 [2008] IRLR 187 (EAT)

4 This is considered in more detail in **Chapter 2**

5 This is considered in more detail in **Chapter 3**

Regulation 3(4)(c) is silent on SPCs, there should be no reason in principle why an SPC could not occur where most of the staff are in Great Britain, but a few employees assigned to the relevant activities work abroad. This is the view taken in the BIS Guide and it must be correct[6].

- Post-transfer: The fact that the business or services will be conducted overseas may, of itself, be an indicator that the relevant economic entity does not retain its identity under Regulation 3(1)(a) and/or the activities to be performed are not fundamentally the same under Regulation 3(1)(b). This will be fact-specific.

It does not matter that: (a) the relevant contractual arrangements effecting the transfer; and/or (b) the employment of individuals employed in the organised grouping of resources or employees are governed by the laws of another country[7].

Redundancies and relocations

Where a business or services is moving from the UK to another country, the overseas transferee will need to consider how best to manage the transferor's UK-based workforce.

In most circumstances, it will be treated as a place of work redundancy, but this is not always straightforward.

The transferee may want such redundancies to take place pre-transfer, particularly if it does not have any existing presence in the UK. However, this is difficult under TUPE because even if the transferor is willing to co-operate, it cannot dismiss employees pre-transfer and rely on the transferee's ETO reason. For employees with at least two years' service, this inevitably leads to an automatic unfair dismissal.

---

6 BIS Guide, page 14

7 Regulation 3(4)(b)

It is possible to deal with this pragmatically. The transferor could approach employees who are in scope to transfer and offer them two options. They can object to the transfer and accept enhanced redundancy terms under a settlement agreement (under which they waive claims against both transferor and transferee). Alternatively, they can choose to transfer and take their chances on any redundancy process that the transferee may follow, noting that the terms offered post-transfer may be less generous.

This approach may be suitable for intra-group transfers, where a company is moving operations to one of its own overseas subsidiaries and does not wish to offer redeployment overseas.

It may not be possible where the transferor is unwilling to co-operate. In those cases, the transferee may be forced to follow a UK redundancy process, post-transfer. There may be practical issues to overcome, if the transferor refuses to allow the employees continued access to its premises or the site is shut down. The employees may simply be asked to work from home (if possible) or at a transferee's site nearby (if any). Otherwise, they may simply be asked not to work but remain on full pay, pending the outcome of redundancy consultation.

The alternative, of course, is for the transferee to move the employees overseas and eventually make them redundant there. However, this will rarely be practical. Quite apart from the logistical effort involved in moving (potentially unwanted) employees to another part of the world, there may be complicated arguments over whether English or local employment law applies to any dismissal. It will usually be better to make a firm decision on resourcing at the outset and deal with any necessary redundancies in the UK.

There may be circumstances where an employee asks to relocate. If the transferee does not want to take them on, it may be able to argue that a role in another country is not a suitable alternative, even if it is roughly equivalent to the employee's existing UK-based role. However, this would need to be considered as part of redundancy consultation.

If the transferee is willing to continue employing them overseas, it can likely do so on local terms of employment (on the basis that there is a valid ETO reason for varying terms and conditions). In *Xerox Business Services Philippines Inc Ltd v. Zeb*[8], the EAT rejected an argument that an employee could seek to relocate from the UK to the Philippines but rely on TUPE to preserve his more generous UK terms. The employer had never offered this option and, in effect, the employee was seeking to vary his contract unilaterally. The correct approach is to treat it as a place of work redundancy and then consider whether the new role (on local terms) is a suitable alternative.

An employee might also seek to pre-empt any redundancy process by resigning and bringing a claim under Regulation 4(9) or 4(11). If they are concerned about the ability to enforce any claims against an overseas transferee, they may be better served in objecting to the transfer and claiming under Regulation 4(11) – as liability will then remain with the transferor under *University of Oxford v. Humphreys*[9]. However, they would still need to convince a Tribunal that the proposal to relocate work overseas amounted to a repudiatory breach of contract by their employer.

For individuals who are assigned to the relevant UK-based undertaking (or British-based services) but work abroad, there is a question over whether they are entitled to rely on and enforce TUPE protections and associated rights (such as unfair dismissal) in the UK. The Regulations are unhelpfully silent, so it will likely depend on case law principles under which the employee must be able to establish a stronger connection to Great Britain and British employment law than their base country[10].

8 [2018] IRLR 495

9 [2000] IRLR 183 (CA) – see **Chapter 8** for a detailed discussion

10 See *Serco Ltd v. Lawson* [2006] IRLR 289 (HL) and subsequent UK Supreme Court authorities on the territoriality of UK statutory employment protection – e.g. *Ravat v. Halliburton Manufacturing and Services Ltd* [2012] IRLR 315 (UKSC) and *Duncombe and ors v. Secretary*

This is likely to be a relatively high hurdle. However, they could potentially have a remedy under the laws of their home country if, for example, the transfer results in the termination of their employment. More generally, any dispute relating to their employment contract may give rise to potential choice of law and jurisdiction issues, particularly if the contract is silent. These are beyond the scope of this book, but will need careful consideration and local law advice.

Transfers from or between overseas countries

TUPE will not apply where the organised grouping of resources or employees is based overseas, immediately before the transfer. However, analogous protections may apply in a foreign jurisdiction, where the business operations, assets or activities are to be transferred to the UK or another country.

For example, all EU member states will have domestic laws based on the ARD, which will apply to the transfer of an economic entity. However, the ARD provides a relatively loose framework of overarching minimum requirements, which each member state has interpreted and transposed in its own way.

It is also worth remembering that in outsourcing scenarios, unlike the UK, EU member states do not have separate regimes related to service provision changes. Therefore, local transfer legislation may be less likely to apply to an outsourcing scenario, whether it occurs within the relevant EU member state or results in a potential transfer to the UK (or elsewhere). It may depend simply on whether there is a transfer of an undertaking, based on the *Spijkers* test and local case law.

Similarly, some countries outside the EU will have varying degrees of protection for employees on the sale or transfer of a business or an

---

of State for Children, Schools and Families [2011] IRLR 840 (UKSC) – for a full discussion of this complex issue

outsourcing (whether underpinned by local law or simply as a matter of commercial practice). These should be checked at the very outset.

Practical considerations

The level of protection, procedural requirements and available remedies for employees will vary considerably between countries. This will need to be reflected in the commercial agreement between the parties and the overall transaction timescales.

For example:

1. Where multiple countries are involved, there may be separate country-specific agreements or schedules dealing with employee transfers which are incorporated into an overarching master agreement and require negotiation at local level.

2. The minimum timeframes for information and consultation with employee representatives may differ across countries. There may be applicable collective bargaining agreements to consider and/or an obligation to engage with works councils or unions at an early stage. It will be important to co-ordinate the timing of consultation and associated employee communications across countries.

3. Works councils, unions or other employee representative bodies may also dictate the pace of consultation and potentially act as a significant blocker. A failure to follow the correct local procedures or perceived lack of good faith could lead to considerable delay. The relationships between the relevant local business, the employee representatives and the wider workforce will be important in resolving any potential sticking points.

4. Employees may also be entitled to enhanced termination payments under local law. Further, an unlawful termination of employment because of or connected to the transfer might lead

to reinstatement in some jurisdictions, rather than simply compensation. This creates potentially heightened commercial risks for transferor and/or transferee.

5. In some countries, there is no statutory requirement for the transferor to provide minimum employee information to the transferee. This may cause practical difficulties in assessing what the transferee may inherit and the issues that may require pre-transfer consultation. Further, the circumstances in which terms of employment may be harmonised post-transfer can vary, depending on local laws.

The management of TUPE projects in general is considered in more detail in **Chapter 20**.

CHAPTER TWENTY

MANAGING A TUPE PROJECT

There is no universal blueprint that can be applied to all TUPE scenarios. Every TUPE project will have its own unique quirks. Each party will have its commercial objectives and red lines; unexpected problems will arise through due diligence (or lack of it); and issues arising from consultation can throw a spanner in the works of an otherwise beautifully negotiated agreement.

However, it is useful to provide some basic structure for a business confronted with a potential TUPE transfer, whether arising from a business sale or an SPC. Most projects can be broken down into five steps:

- Step 1: Prepare
- Step 2: Bid and negotiate
- Step 3: Consult and communicate
- Step 4: Transition
- Step 5: Integrate

Typically, Steps 1 to 3 will take place before the relevant transfer. Step 4 may straddle pre- and post-transfer and Step 5 is usually post-transfer. However, there will likely be some flexibility and overlap, depending on the nature of the transaction.

Step 1: Prepare

This is the most important stage of all. Poor preparation often leads to unpleasant surprises, unanticipated consequences, additional costs and delay.

The commercial checklists in **Chapter 21** provide guidance on practical questions to consider. The aim should be to answer as many of these as possible, at the initial planning stage. It will help to map out Steps 2 to 5.

Why are you doing it?

For the prospective buyer and seller of a business, consider the overall commercial objective of the deal and how TUPE might (or might not) assist in achieving it. Employees will rarely be the only factor in play, but could be an important one. The transfer or otherwise of employees could have a material bearing on the cost, timing and overall value of the deal. The willingness or ability of a seller to offer warranties or indemnities may dictate price.

Similarly, a customer involved in a potential SPC will want to think about why it is proposing to outsource, insource or re-tender activities. The transfer of employees may be counter-productive, where it does not want the same people doing the same work. Equally, the non-transfer of employees could leave an unwelcome void, if they have specialist skills or extensive knowledge that remains valuable for continuity and quality of service.

A prospective service provider bidding for a contract will also need to consider carefully what a successful bid looks like. Is the scope of the services within its existing capabilities and aligned with its strategy? Will it want or need additional staff or skills to fulfil the services? If there is no TUPE transfer, where will they get them?

The project team

Be clear at the outset on the division of internal responsibility and any relevant decision-making processes. This is particularly important for large-scale projects (where there may be multiple workstreams across multiple countries) or in larger organisations.

For example, an outsourcing may involve procurement, in-house legal (both commercial and employment), HR and the relevant business unit utilising the services. Specialist project managers or external consultants may be brought in. Local HR and country managers may need to co-ordinate activity on the ground and liaise with unions and works councils. They might also be impacted personally by the proposed transfer.

Effective communication channels, centralised project management and a clear decision-making and reporting structure should be established quickly.

Where a commercial call needs to be taken by "the business", there should be no ambiguity about who has authority to take that decision.

The importance of due diligence

Any incoming employer will need to assess what it might be getting, if TUPE applies. Ideally, it should have clear understanding of how many employees may be involved, where they are based, the associated staffing costs, what terms of employment they have and any significant liabilities. It can then start to match this information up against its existing workforce, work out what it actually needs and prepare a negotiation strategy.

In a corporate transaction, this can usually be achieved by submitting a due diligence questionnaire. Where there are multiple bids for a proposed business purchase, the seller may dictate what information is shared.

For a seller or customer, it makes sense to provide as much information as possible, as early as possible (within the confines of data protection obligations). Any material levels of uncertainty may be factored into the purchase price or cost of the services.

Equally, in some cases, a putative transferee may need to accept that information may be limited. An outgoing service provider that is under no contractual obligation to disclose anything in advance may stick doggedly to the scope and timing of statutory employee liability information requirements. A replacement provider may have to take a degree of risk and hedge it by negotiating indemnity protection or a price adjustment mechanism, if it wants to remain competitive on price.

An incoming employer should also not underestimate the costs of any relocation or restructuring that may be needed, post-transfer. This may make the whole enterprise less profitable, at least for a while.

Be realistic on timing

It is sensible to build a significant time buffer into your project plan.

Projects which are run to very tight, inflexible schedules will usually result in heightened risk (for example, because the consultation process is compromised or corners have been cut in negotiations or due diligence). This may be an acceptable trade-off in some cases, but arbitrary deadlines should be avoided where possible.

Electing employee representatives can take time and controversial or unpopular measures can lead to protracted discussions. Multi-jurisdictional projects are often more complex, because of the varying requirements of local laws and customs[1].

It may not be straightforward to implement significant change overnight. For example, if the work is to be relocated, this needs careful planning. The new employer may be juggling place of work

[1] See **Chapter 19**

redundancies for transferring staff alongside hiring new employees to meet service requirements at the new location.

Step 2: Bid and negotiate

Once the initial preparation has been done, it is time for the parties to talk.

In some cases, there will be a bidding process. The customer or seller may issue a request for proposal (or "RFP") and invite selected bidders to tender for the purchase of the business or provision of the services. This may be a closed process (where none of the bidders is aware of how its competitors have priced or scoped out the services). The customer or seller may also dictate the terms at the outset by asking prospective suitors to bid against a draft transactional or services agreement, with limited opportunity to negotiate.

In many cases, there will be an opportunity for meaningful discussion on price, resourcing of services, warranties and transfer indemnities.

Battle lines may be drawn regarding whether or not TUPE applies (and if so, to whom). It makes sense for the parties to resolve any differences on this at an early stage, by agreeing commercial terms. If they persist in presenting conflicting positions, it makes Steps 3 to 5 difficult to manage. Ultimately, employees may find themselves caught between two potential employers, neither of whom accepts responsibility for them. They may have no option but to claim against both parties. Either TUPE is engaged or it isn't, so one of them has to be wrong.

Often, a customer will also invite the incumbent service provider to bid as part of a re-tendering process. This may seem counter-intuitive, as re-tenders are usually driven by a level of dissatisfaction with the current services. However, it can be an effective tool for renegotiating commercial terms and driving efficiencies. The incumbent does have some advantages over its rivals. It is already in situ, aware of the customer's requirements and will likely have the right size and structure of workforce to be able to manage the services, with minimal disruption. Going with what you know involves less upheaval.

Step 3: Consult and communicate

Once principal commercial terms have been agreed and a putative transfer date is set, the information and consultation process can begin[2].

For service provision changes, commencement will normally be agreed for a future date that allows for meaningful consultation and business planning. For business sales, this may take place between exchange and completion. However, as noted above, the parties need to build in sufficient time to do this and different procedural requirements may apply outside the UK.

The transferor should also ensure that it has complied with the strict requirements of Regulation 11, by providing up-to-date employee liability information[3]. It should not simply assume that this box has already been ticked, where information has already been disclosed at an earlier stage.

If TUPE does not apply, it may still be necessary to each party to engage with its respective workforce, where a business sale or outsourcing affects work levels or working conditions. A business sale or the loss of a contract may result in redundancies. Conversely, a successful bid to provide services that does not bring employees with it under TUPE may result in increased workloads for the new provider's existing staff.

Either way, the importance of timely communication with employees and their representatives cannot be overstated. Change is often unsettling for those at the coalface. An information vacuum is often filled with speculation and rumour, which can be damaging. It is

---

2 See **Chapter 17**

3 See **Chapter 16**

usually much better for the employer to keep control of the narrative with straightforward, open dialogue and by creating a space for employees to ask questions.

Step 4: Transition

This stage involves getting ready for the post-transaction environment, regardless of whether TUPE applies. It will usually overlap with Step 3.

This could mean one or more of the following:

- Redeployment – employees who are not transferring may need to be moved to other projects or business areas. This may be phased in over a period of time, depending on the extent to which an employee is required to continue working on the transferring business or services (or otherwise involved in managing the transition process itself).

- Redundancies – employees who are left behind may be surplus to requirements and therefore at risk of redundancy. Employees who are otherwise in scope to transfer but not required by the transferee may be approached pre-transfer about prospective redundancy terms[4]. The transferee may commence collective redundancy consultation before the transfer, alongside (but separate to) the TUPE consultation process[5]. It may also need to consider whether to include some of its existing employees in post-transfer redundancy pooling and begin preparations accordingly.

- Managing transitional arrangements – an outsourcing agreement may prescribe detailed steps to facilitate a smooth handover to a new provider and minimise service disruption. It may involve a gradual ramp-down of activities by the transferor

4 See **Chapter 19** for a discussion on how this is managed in practice

5 See **Chapter 17**

and consequent ramp-up by the transferee. This will likely span any TUPE transfer itself.

- HR operations – there will be some important housekeeping to do in relation to any transferring staff. The transferor will usually need to issue P45s and remove the employees from its payroll, even though employment is not terminating. Arrangements should be made to transfer personnel records, with particular care taken to ensure compliance with data protection obligations.

  The transferee should satisfy itself that all transferring employees have the right to work in the UK. This is in accordance with the Home Office's *Employer's guide to right to work checks*, which allows a grace period of 60 days from the transfer date. Although it is able to rely on immigration checks performed by the transferor, it will also inherit liability for illegal workers. A warranty from the transferor may bring some comfort, but it does not provide a defence.

  Separate background checks may also be required by a customer (even for the transferee's existing staff), as part of the deal. Failure to satisfy these would not, however, prevent an employee from transferring under TUPE.

Step 5: Integrate

The post-transfer integration of transferring staff into the transferee's existing workforce requires careful management.

Some employees may have preferred not to move and feel caught up in events beyond their control. There should be a well-planned communication and onboarding strategy to make them feel welcome. Changes in management structure and reporting lines should be handled sensitively. Where possible, it may make sense to absorb transferring employees into the transferee's existing teams gradually, if that is the ultimate intention. A period of acclimatisation can help to calm any jitters.

Similarly, existing staff may feel threatened by new arrivals. They might have better terms and conditions, which the transferee is required to honour but can cause consternation amongst its long-serving employees. They may also do similar types of work and even if there are no immediate post-transfer redundancies planned, some may perceive the writing to be on the wall and start looking elsewhere.

In either scenario, valuable staff who are flight risks should be identified quickly and reassured. Retention incentives might be considered in appropriate cases.

Longer term, the transferee may seek to harmonise terms and conditions, once it is confident that this can be distanced from the transfer itself.

CHAPTER TWENTY-ONE

OUTSOURCING: COMMERCIAL CHECKLISTS

So let's bring everything together. Here are some basic commercial questions that the relevant parties involved in a potential service provision change should be considering at the outset.

I have looked at this separately from the perspective of each of the transferor, the transferee and a customer who is neither of these (where services are moving from one provider to another). There is inevitably some overlap.

Many of these questions will apply equally to the buyer and seller negotiating a transactional agreement for the sale and purchase of a business or assets.

The big question

"Do you want TUPE to apply?"

This is the first and most important HR-related issue to consider for any party involved in a potential outsourcing scenario. A focus on the preferred outcome (regardless of whether TUPE will actually be engaged) will drive the approach to commercial negotiations, both in relation to the immediate SPC at hand and any future anticipated SPC.

For the customer, it is crucial to understand the underlying business objective for outsourcing, insourcing or re-tendering the work in the first place. Is it the quality of the service? Cost? Efficiency? A combination of all of these, to varying degrees?

If the customer is dissatisfied with the standard of services being delivered by the existing provider's staff, the last thing it may want is for the same individuals to report for work at the new provider, after the transfer. The uniform may be different, but the quality may not improve.

Conversely, maintaining a consistent workforce may be integral, particularly if certain employees have specialised skills or a deep knowledge of the customer's requirements or systems. In these cases, TUPE can be used to ensure continuity and preserve existing employment terms.

Sometimes, the customer may wish to have the best of all worlds, by cherry-picking certain employees and leaving others behind. This is not always straightforward to achieve simply by applying TUPE principles and it may cost more, but a negotiated commercial solution can often be found with willingness on all sides.

Or the customer may, of course, be largely ambivalent about employee issues. If the overriding factor is greater efficiency in how the services are provided (for example, through better technology or automation), the longer-term human resources requirements may assume less importance. Again, this may impact how hard it negotiates on TUPE issues, relative to other commercial aspects of the deal.

Any outgoing or new service provider should also be addressing its mind to this issue, at the earliest stage. Being lumbered with employees for whom it does not have sufficient work (or losing very valuable employees in which it has invested and trained up) may dictate its strategy.

As we have already seen, much of the argument around whether TUPE applies will focus on whether the new services are *"fundamentally the same"* and/or whether there is an *"organised grouping of employees"*[1]. However, it is important to remember that an outsourcing, insourcing

1 See **Chapter 3**

or re-tendering process could still potentially be a transfer of an economic entity under Regulation 3(1)(a), even if it does not meet the requirements of an SPC under Regulation 3(1)(b).

For outgoing employers

The outgoing employer (or transferor) will be either: (a) the customer, where activities are currently performed in-house and therefore being outsourced for the first time; or (b) an incumbent service provider, where services are being re-tendered and activities are moving to a new service provider. This could include any sub-contractor engaged by the principal incumbent service provider.

What is the potential impact of services terminating?

- If TUPE applies, who is assigned to the relevant organised grouping of resources or employees (and will therefore transfer out)? Can anyone be redeployed pre-transfer, to avoid them being assigned at the point of transfer?
- How will you replace any key employees who transfer out (and any associated lost skills or experience)? Are you prepared for valuable staff to transfer to a competitor? Will you need to recruit (and, if so, in what timescale)?
- If TUPE does not apply, how will you manage any employees who worked on the account? Can they be redeployed elsewhere in the business? Are potential redundancies envisaged (and if so, might they impact the wider workforce)?
- Is there a knock-on impact on any sub-contractor arrangements? How should this be managed?

Incumbent service providers: What does the contract say?

- What employee information are you required to provide to the customer? When?
- Are you restricted in how you manage your workforce? For example, are you prevented from moving employees to and from other projects or clients?
- What are your obligations in relation to arranging a smooth transition of services?
- What is the potential cost of any indemnity protection provided to the customer or a replacement service provider?

What is the TUPE process?

- To the extent not already done, have you complied with your obligation to provide employee liability information?
- Do you need to arrange for the election of representatives for the transferring employees, for the purposes of information and consultation?
- Will any of your other employees potentially be affected by the transfer? If so, do separate representatives need to be elected for them?
- Do you have all the information required to be provided to employee representatives? Remember that this includes certain information regarding agency workers. Has the transferee provided sufficiently detailed information on measures?
- How will any necessary consultation in relation to such measures be conducted? Will you allow the transferee to engage directly with representatives of transferring employees?

- If potential collective redundancies may result from the transfer, will you allow the transferee to start pre-transfer redundancy consultation?

For incoming employers

The incoming employer (or transferee) will be either: (a) the customer, where activities are currently performed by an incumbent service provider and being brought in-house; or (b) a new service provider, where activities are currently performed by the customer itself or an incumbent service provider. Again, this could include sub-contractors, where the principal new service provider proposes to farm out some of the services it is contracting to perform.

What might you get?

- Who is likely to transfer? How much do they cost and where are they based?

- Are there other potential transferees (for example, where more than one new service provider is appointed)? Might this result in employees' time being split between providers under separate part-time employment contracts (or additional termination costs)?

- What employment terms might be inherited? Are there any particularly generous benefits or perks (whether contractual or otherwise), unusually long notice periods, potential "Beckmann" liabilities under an occupational pension scheme or enhanced redundancy schemes?

- How do existing benefits align with what you provide to your existing workforce? Remember that changing terms or harmonising benefits may be difficult to achieve.

- Are there any existing or threatened claims relating to transferring employees? If so, seek additional information that will enable you to take advice on their merits and quantum.

- Do any transferring employees have the right level of skills or experience to perform the services that are being offered? If not, will they need additional training? Do they have strong relationships with key contacts at the customer which are worth preserving?

- Does the customer have any views on specific transferring employees who should be: (a) incentivised to remain; or (b) moved off the account (and potentially dismissed, if they cannot be redeployed)? Who will pay for this?

- Are there any indemnities or other protections in an existing services agreement, which the customer can pass on to you (or which can be enforced by you directly)?

<u>What will you need?</u>

- How many employees are required to perform the work (and in what roles)? Where will they be based? Will there be a change in work location that results in redundancies and the need to hire elsewhere?

- Will you have too many employees? If so, how and when will any redundancies be managed? What are the potential costs and who will pay for them? Can you persuade the customer that a limited transfer of staff will achieve costs savings without impacting service delivery?

- If TUPE does not apply, will there be sufficient capacity within your current workforce to deliver the services?

- Will you need to recruit additional staff, to fill any skills or knowledge gaps? What is the likely timescale for this?

- Are there any key transferring employees who represent a potential flight risk? How should this be managed?

How will you operate?

- How will the work be organised? Will there be a key account manager or, more broadly, a specific team deliberately put together to perform the contracted services for the customer? Will certain employees be assigned to that team?

- Will you seek to sub-contract any part of the services?

- What transitional arrangements will be put in place, with either the customer or any outgoing service provider?

- How might the commercial dynamic between you and the outgoing service provider affect any transfer process or transitional arrangements? Are they likely to be uncooperative and, if so, should that be discussed with the customer at the outset?

What is the TUPE process?

- Will any of your existing employees potentially be affected by the transfer? If so, do you need to arrange for the election of employee representatives, for the purposes of information and consultation?

- What measures might you propose in relation to transferring employees?

- How will any necessary consultation in relation to such measures be conducted? Will you have the opportunity to engage directly with representatives of transferring employees?

- If potential collective redundancies may result from the transfer, will you seek to agree a means of starting pre-transfer redundancy consultation with the outgoing employer?

- Will the outgoing employee provide full details of employment contracts and personnel records at the point of transfer (to the extent these have not already been received)?

For re-tendering customers

Where activities are moving from an incumbent to a new service provider, the customer will be neither transferor nor transferee. It will be an onlooker to any TUPE transfer, but in many cases it will likely want significant input into how the transition is managed and how future services are resourced.

<u>How do you manage the change in service provider?</u>

- What does the existing services contract say about how any potential employment liabilities will be managed on termination? What are the potential costs? Can the benefit and burden of any indemnities be passed to the new service provider?

- If TUPE does not apply, who will bear any redundancy costs? Will these be factored into the overall pricing of the services, regardless of indemnity provisions?

- What information is the incumbent service provider obliged to give, for the purposes of a re-tendering process? Will they be invited to re-tender?

- How much time will be needed to re-tender services, appoint a new provider and carry out any necessary consultation?

- If more than one new provider is being appointed, does that cause potential complications with employment contracts being split?

- What transitional arrangements will be necessary to ensure a smooth handover and continuity of service? Does the existing contract specify any protocols that the incumbent service provider should follow? Should the contract with the new provider specify what it must do to assist in any transition?

- Where will the new service provider perform the services? Will a change in location cause delay and additional costs in making employees redundant and rehiring elsewhere?

- What is the potential financial and commercial cost of any disruption that may be caused by changing providers? Will it have any impact on your own employees (for example, anyone currently managing the relationship with the incumbent service provider or dealing with them locally)? Is it less disruptive to re-appoint the incumbent provider, but use a re-tendering process to drive better commercial terms?

How much control do you need?

- Who will actually perform the services? Will the new service provider be permitted to sub-contract some or all of the work?

- Are there any key staff who must transfer to the new provider (and, if necessary, incentivised to stay in the longer-term? Are there any transferring employees who must be moved off the account?

- How will the work be organised by the new provider? Do you need a dedicated account manager or core cohort of key staff to perform the services?

- Do you need the right to "vet or veto" key staff who will be providing the services? Are any background checks required?

- What information should the new service provider be required to provide to you about the employees performing the work? How often?

- What happens on termination of future services? Do you envisage moving the services to another new provider, or is it possible that they might be brought in-house? Should the new service provider be restricted in how it manages its staff, in the lead-up to termination?

POSTSCRIPT

TUPE POST-BREXIT: WHAT NEXT?

During the course of writing this book, the UK Government (rather unsportingly, in my view) proposed new draft legislation which may have a profound impact on TUPE. Indeed, its very existence may be under threat.

As I write this in late-January 2023, the Retained EU Law (Revocation and Reform) Bill is making its way through Parliament.

If adopted into law in its current form, it would mean that any UK regulations derived from EU law will be automatically revoked at the end of 2023, unless a specific decision is taken to keep them. This seems to be an artificial and unrealistic deadline. There is scope to extend it to 23 June 2026 (symbolically, the 10-year anniversary of the Brexit vote), although there is no guarantee that this will happen.

At its most extreme, it could mean the immediate repeal of swathes of employment regulation implemented by virtue of the UK's membership of the EU – including TUPE.

However, even this is not straightforward. TUPE contains a mixture of provisions based on the minimum requirements of the ARD and further gold-plated protections that have no basis in EU law (such as the rules relating to service provision changes). If no action is taken and the axe is brought down on the EU-derived laws relating to a transfer of an economic entity, it is unclear to what extent the SPC regime might survive.

Alternatively, nothing could happen at all. Parliament could decide to preserve TUPE in its existing form, perhaps with one eye on potential future reform. This is perhaps more likely. It is difficult to predict what alterations might be made, although the UK Government's emphasis on boosting innovation in our economy and attracting investment may lend itself to a relaxation of certain employee protections. In that context, I can see the attraction of making post-transfer harmonisation of terms and conditions more straightforward and consultation requirements less prescriptive.

Assuming TUPE does survive in one form or another, it could be interpreted in a very different way in the future. The current version of the Bill abolishes the supremacy of EU law, although Parliament could choose to preserve this principle in particular instances.

In a worst-case scenario, it leaves a potential legal vacuum. All the previous European case law on which our domestic courts have relied so heavily in interpreting TUPE would have no bearing on how future cases might be decided. It may be helpful in certain instances (such as allowing courts to sidestep *Govaerts*) but overall it will only create uncertainty. You only need to look down the List of Cases at the front of this book to see what a profound impact this might have, seemingly overnight.

So we wait and see. It is entirely possible that the next edition of this book will be radically different to the first. If that is the case, I hope it will be the result of carefully considered legal reform, rather than an ill-considered rush job as TUPE is caught up in a wider political zeal to slash EU red tape and "get Brexit done".

MORE BOOKS BY LAW BRIEF PUBLISHING

A selection of our other titles available now:-

'A Practical Guide to Hoarding and Mental Health for Housing Lawyers' by Rachel Coyle
'A Practical Guide to Psychiatric Claims in Personal Injury – 2nd Edition' by Liam Ryan
'Stephens on Contractual Indemnities' by Richard Stephens
'A Practical Guide to the EU Succession Regulation' by Richard Frimston
'A Practical Guide to Solicitor and Client Costs – 2nd Edition' by Robin Dunne
'Constructive Dismissal – Practice Pointers and Principles' by Benjimin Burgher
'A Practical Guide to Religion and Belief Discrimination Claims in the Workplace' by Kashif Ali
'A Practical Guide to the Law of Medical Treatment Decisions' by Ben Troke
'Fundamental Dishonesty and QOCS in Personal Injury Proceedings: Law and Practice' by Jake Rowley
'A Practical Guide to the Law in Relation to School Exclusions' by Charlotte Hadfield & Alice de Coverley
'A Practical Guide to Divorce for the Silver Separators' by Karin Walker
'The Right to be Forgotten – The Law and Practical Issues' by Melissa Stock
'A Practical Guide to Planning Law and Rights of Way in National Parks, the Broads and AONBs' by James Maurici QC, James Neill et al
'A Practical Guide to Election Law' by Tom Tabori
'A Practical Guide to the Law in Relation to Surrogacy' by Andrew Powell
'A Practical Guide to Claims Arising from Fatal Accidents – 2nd Edition' by James Patience
'A Practical Guide to the Ownership of Employee Inventions – From Entitlement to Compensation' by James Tumbridge & Ashley Roughton
'A Practical Guide to Asbestos Claims' by Jonathan Owen & Gareth McAloon
'A Practical Guide to Stamp Duty Land Tax in England and Northern Ireland' by Suzanne O'Hara
'A Practical Guide to the Law of Farming Partnerships' by Philip Whitcomb
'Covid-19, Homeworking and the Law – The Essential Guide to Employment and GDPR Issues' by Forbes Solicitors
'Covid-19 and Criminal Law – The Essential Guide' by Ramya Nagesh
'Covid-19 and Family Law in England and Wales – The Essential Guide' by Safda Mahmood

'A Practical Guide to the Law of Unlawful Eviction and Harassment – 2nd Edition' by Stephanie Lovegrove
'Covid-19, Brexit and the Law of Commercial Leases – The Essential Guide' by Mark Shelton
'A Practical Guide to Costs in Personal Injury Claims – 2nd Edition' by Matthew Hoe
'A Practical Guide to the General Data Protection Regulation (GDPR) – 2nd Edition' by Keith Markham
'Ellis on Credit Hire – Sixth Edition' by Aidan Ellis & Tim Kevan
'A Practical Guide to Working with Litigants in Person and McKenzie Friends in Family Cases' by Stuart Barlow
'Protecting Unregistered Brands: A Practical Guide to the Law of Passing Off' by Lorna Brazell
'A Practical Guide to Secondary Liability and Joint Enterprise Post-Jogee' by Joanne Cecil & James Mehigan
'A Practical Guide to the Pre-Action RTA Claims Protocol for Personal Injury Lawyers' by Antonia Ford
'A Practical Guide to Neighbour Disputes and the Law' by Alexander Walsh
'A Practical Guide to Forfeiture of Leases' by Mark Shelton
'A Practical Guide to Coercive Control for Legal Practitioners and Victims' by Rachel Horman
'A Practical Guide to Rights Over Airspace and Subsoil' by Daniel Gatty
'Tackling Disclosure in the Criminal Courts – A Practitioner's Guide' by Narita Bahra QC & Don Ramble
'A Practical Guide to the Law of Driverless Cars – Second Edition' by Alex Glassbrook, Emma Northey & Scarlett Milligan
'A Practical Guide to TOLATA Claims' by Greg Williams
'A Practical Guide to Elderly Law – 2nd Edition' by Justin Patten
'A Practical Guide to Responding to Housing Disrepair and Unfitness Claims' by Iain Wightwick
'A Practical Guide to the Construction and Rectification of Wills and Trust Instruments' by Edward Hewitt
'A Practical Guide to the Law of Bullying and Harassment in the Workplace' by Philip Hyland
'How to Be a Freelance Solicitor: A Practical Guide to the SRA-Regulated Freelance Solicitor Model' by Paul Bennett

'A Practical Guide to Prison Injury Claims' by Malcolm Johnson
'A Practical Guide to the Small Claims Track - 2nd Edition' by Dominic Bright
'A Practical Guide to Advising Clients at the Police Station' by Colin Stephen McKeown-Beaumont
'A Practical Guide to Antisocial Behaviour Injunctions' by Iain Wightwick
'Practical Mediation: A Guide for Mediators, Advocates, Advisers, Lawyers, and Students in Civil, Commercial, Business, Property, Workplace, and Employment Cases' by Jonathan Dingle with John Sephton
'The Mini-Pupillage Workbook' by David Boyle
'A Practical Guide to Crofting Law' by Brian Inkster
'A Practical Guide to Spousal Maintenance' by Liz Cowell
'A Practical Guide to the Law of Domain Names and Cybersquatting' by Andrew Clemson
'A Practical Guide to the Law of Gender Pay Gap Reporting' by Harini Iyengar
'A Practical Guide to the Rights of Grandparents in Children Proceedings' by Stuart Barlow
'NHS Whistleblowing and the Law' by Joseph England
'Employment Law and the Gig Economy' by Nigel Mackay & Annie Powell
'A Practical Guide to Noise Induced Hearing Loss (NIHL) Claims' by Andrew Mckie, Ian Skeate, Gareth McAloon
'An Introduction to Beauty Negligence Claims – A Practical Guide for the Personal Injury Practitioner' by Greg Almond
'Intercompany Agreements for Transfer Pricing Compliance' by Paul Sutton
'Zen and the Art of Mediation' by Martin Plowman
'A Practical Guide to the SRA Principles, Individual and Law Firm Codes of Conduct 2019 – What Every Law Firm Needs to Know' by Paul Bennett
'A Practical Guide to Adoption for Family Lawyers' by Graham Pegg
'A Practical Guide to Industrial Disease Claims' by Andrew Mckie & Ian Skeate
'A Practical Guide to Redundancy' by Philip Hyland
'A Practical Guide to Vicarious Liability' by Mariel Irvine
'A Practical Guide to Applications for Landlord's Consent and Variation of Leases' by Mark Shelton
'A Practical Guide to Relief from Sanctions Post-Mitchell and Denton' by Peter Causton

www.ingramcontent.com/pod-product-compliance
Lightning Source LLC
LaVergne TN
LVHW052306200926
848481LV00002B/475

* 9 7 8 1 9 1 4 6 0 8 4 8 3 *